THE NEW JAPANESE ARCHITECTURE

Takefumi Aida, Kazama House, Kawaguchi, 1987

THE NEW
JAPANESE ARCHITECTURE

Botond Bognar

Introduction by John Morris Dixon

Essays by Hajime Yatsuka and Lynne Breslin

First published in the United States of America in 1990
by RIZZOLI INTERNATIONAL PUBLICATIONS, INC.
300 Park Avenue South, New York, NY 10010

Library of Congress Cataloging-in-Publication Data

Bognar, Botond, 1944–
    The new Japanese architecture / Botond Bognar :
introduction by John Morris Dixon.
        p.   cm.
    ISBN 0-8478-1225-1. — ISBN 0-8478-1266-9 (pbk.)
    1. Architecture, Modern—20th century—Japan.
    2. Architecture—Japan.   I. Title.
NA   1555.B54   1990
720'.952'09045—dc20   90-8395
                                                          CIP

Designed by Paul Chevannes
Typeset by Rainsford Type, Danbury, Ct
Printed and bound in Japan

Front cover: Itsuko Hasegawa, Shonandai Cultural Center, Fujisawa City, 1989 (photo); Hiromi Fujii, Ushimado International Arts Festival Center, 1985
(axonometric).
Back cover (hardcover only) : Kazuyo Sejima, Platform,
Katsuura, Chiba Prefecture, 1988 (photo).

Illustration Credits

*Numbered illustrations are indicated in italics. All photo-
graphs by B. Bognar except those listed below.*
Tadao Ando, courtesy of: 112 (bottom), 113–15, 119, 126
Masao Arai: 74 (bottom), 75, 76 (bottom), 77, 82 (top), 83
Mitsumasa Fujizaka: *19*
Koji Horiuchi: *20*
Koji Kobayashi: *25*
Akira Komiyama, courtesy of: 190, 191
Kisho Kurokawa, courtesy of: 62, 63
Mitsuo Matsuoka: 122, 123, 125
Ryuji Miyamoto: 214
Tomio Ohashi: 58 (top), 59, 61, 85, 112 (top), 159, 161
S. Ohno: 204, 205
K. Sakamoto: *24*
Shin Takamatsu, courtesy of: 200
Minoru Takeyama, courtesy of: 102 (bottom), 103
Koji Taki: *31*
Kenzo Tange: *3*
R. Yamamoto, courtesy of: 174 (top)

For my wife Binky, and
sons Balazs, Zsolt, and Balint

Acknowledgments

I would like to acknowledge with great appreciation all the help I received from the numerous contributors to this book; they include the architects who provided many of the building descriptions, plus the graphic material and some of the photographs; they further include John Morris Dixon, Lynne Breslin, and Hajime Yatsuka who, responding to my invitation promptly and positively, wrote the Introduction and the accompanying critical essays with much skill and dedication.

Also, I would like to thank the publisher, and especially the editor, David Morton, for his encouragement and numerous suggestions in regard to the material. Vladimir Krstic, Glynis M. Berry, and Keith Krolak contributed some of the project descriptions and I am grateful for their excellent work. In Japan I received invaluable help from my friends, most especially Professor Koji Yagi of TIT, Yasuhiko Matsushiro and his wife Yoshiko Matsushiro, and Nariaki Suzuki (our dear Dōzō Báchi). Thank you.

Furthermore, I thank the director of the School of Architecture, University of Illinois at Urbana-Champaign, Professor Alan Forrester, for his generous support. This book would not have been possible to complete without the kind assistance of the staff of the School, most especially of Jane Cook and Tracy Hawkins who, expertly handling the word processor, typed the whole text over and over while it was in the making.

Last, but not least, I have to acknowledge the substantial contribution of my whole family to this project with their patience and endurance to manage "alone" while I was taking time off for writing and editing; this book therefore is dedicated to my wife and three sons.
B. B.

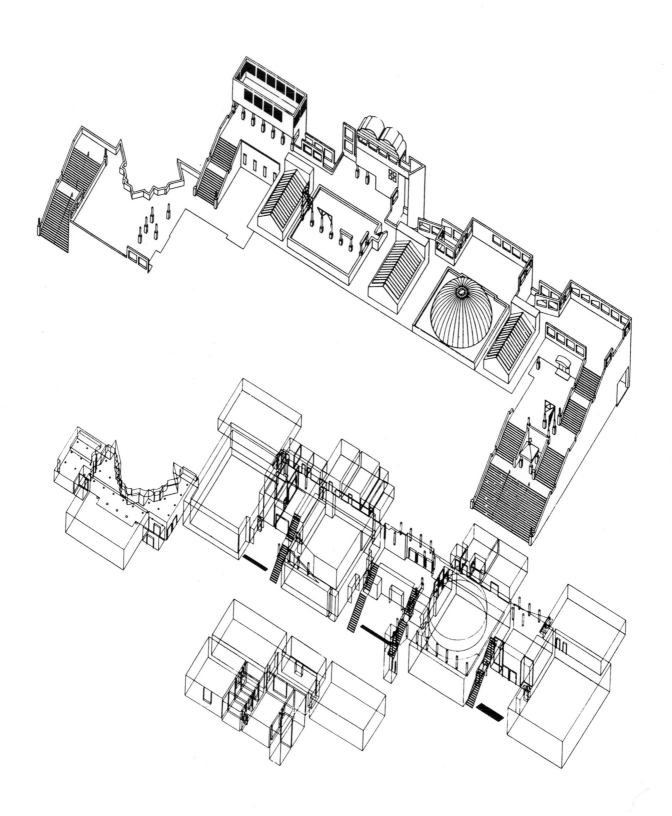

Contents

Foreword

As Japanese architecture approaches the end of the century and that of the millennium, it can look back on an enviably long and rich history as well as an eventful, even stormy and often controversial, recent past. Yet, as a result of its capacity for persistent self-renewal, and achieving maturity, it can by now also reveal qualities and sensibilities that point beyond its previously held singular status of "unique Japaneseness," and mere exotic curiosity or, alternatively, of being a mere "copycat" of Western ideals. Japanese cosmopolitanism, always derivative of a selective but undeniably inclusive attitude, has by now reached a stage where both architecture and design can free themselves from the obligation of paying homage to traditional forms; but, by the same token, they are also able to escape, perhaps for the first time in this century, from the overwhelming gravitational pull of Western domination.[1]

Today, Japan is a superpower not only because of the high level and capacity of its industry and economy, but also due to the originality, predisposition, and influential quality of its design. Hardly, since Japan began trading with the West some one and a half centuries ago, have its applied arts and architecture been so influential abroad—"technically and artistically equal or superior to the architecture and graphic design of any country in the world."[2] The internationalization of, and growing public interest in, architecture are underscored by the fact that an increasing number of foreign architects, including Renzo Piano, Richard Rogers, Frank Gehry, Norman Foster, Zaha Hadid, Michael Graves, Hans Hollein, and others, have found clients in Japan.[3] Through active engagement with the architectural, cultural, economic, and social developments around the globe, many Japanese architects are properly predisposed to address critically important current issues on a global or international level, insofar as these issues in Japan are similar, if not exactly the same, to those that most of the architectural world in Western society faces today. Indeed, if anything, it is these *critical interventions* that are the most remarkable, most challenging aspects of contemporary Japanese architecture, and the ones that most deserve our attention.

Accordingly, the buildings to be introduced on the following pages have been selected with the aim of providing a broad spectrum of important recent examples, that represent such interventions in one way or another. While they embody a wide variety of design intentions, sensibilities and purposes that could appear as different as the buildings themselves, they are similar in two significant aspects: first, all of them make, in a variety of ways, a critical commentary on, or are derivative of, the present day urban and cultural conditions in Japan; second, they all manifest a special fragmentary quality that prevents them from adding up to finished entities and continuous or unified forms. In this architecture, as in the cultural and urban landscape in which these works have been conceived, scattered elements, incongruous motifs and materials, fractional and membranous surfaces, disjunctive forms, and labyrinthine spaces are encountered as liberated and "floating signs" or symbols. Yet, in the best examples, the apparently unrelated and often contradictory parts and patterns, due to some magic or alchemy, seem to hold together unusually well; they are constituted along a unique order, an *integration without synthesis*, where neither opposition nor reconciliation occurs.

By looking at, and more so, by experiencing these works, it becomes increasingly evident that at the end of the century the avant-garde of Japanese architecture is pursuing, at an amazing speed, a path which aims to address and question critically the prevailing Western mode of understanding, definition, and meaning of space, form, and architecture. In reinterpreting certain Japanese architectural themes, these architects are in a process of "deconstructing" the (instrumental) rationality and logic (logocentrism) of Western classical order and metaphysics that have always been predicated on the myth of immutable and dominant laws of a ruling and unimpeachable totality, the unity and absolute presence of a "uni-verse," from which disturbing heterogeneities (the "noise" or the "others") have been systematically expelled. The new *fin-de-siècle* architecture in Japan is thus taking shape at an equidistance from contemporary post-structuralist thought or deconstructionist criticism, the Oriental Japanese mentality of a "floating world," and our highly manipulated and insidiously proliferating present consumer culture, while engaging itself in what may be called, in a Foucaultian sense, "an archaeology of the human consciousness." *B. Bognar*

NOTES
1. Botond Bognar, "An Experiment in 'Orthodox' Architecture with 'Progressive' Aspirations—Nikken Sekkei and the Development of Modern Japanese Architecture," in Botond Bognar and Sandy Heck, *Nikken Sekkei: Building Modern Japan, 1900–1990*, (New York: Princeton Architectural Press, 1990).
2. "Japanese Design: The Golden Age," in *Time* magazine, 21 September, 1987, (Special feature issue), p. 40.
3. There are also a growing number of international competitions in Japan, but for the first time, one has been won by a foreign architect—the one for the Kansai International Airport terminal building in Osaka, won by the Italian Renzo Piano.

INTRODUCTION

Japanese Avant-garde Architects

John Morris Dixon

THIRTY YEARS ago, the idea of an avant-garde Japanese architecture was born. It was in 1960 that a group of young architects put forth their metabolist propositions at the World Design Conference held in Tokyo. Whatever the long-term value of the metabolists' sweeping schemes, they put the West on notice that Japan was, for the first time, making independent contributions to the evolution of modern architecture. From the 1860s through the 1950s, Japanese architects, like their countrymen in industry, had been concerned mainly with learning the ways of the West. There was a glorious Japanese tradition in architecture, as in all the arts, but that had limited application in a nation that had long since become one of the world's most industrialized.

When I first visited Japan, in the mid–1950s, the recovery from the terrible setback of World War II had proceeded far enough and fast enough to produce an air of confidence and hope. As in West Germany, an industrialized society under a regime favorable to economic growth was quickly overcoming the effects of military defeat and physical destruction to regain its high pro-

ductivity and standard of living. The streets of Tokyo were brighter by night than by day; university students and young graduates philosophized in coffee houses where Bach and Chopin were heard through the new wonder of high fidelity. In those days, Japanese businessmen dreamed of owning big black Chryslers, but the streets hummed with locally made two- and three-wheeled vehicles that were the progenitors of today's Hondas and Nissans.

In that period of revived confidence—before the appearance of a recognized avant-garde—some Japanese architects were aspiring to excel their Western idols on their own terms. Kenzo Tange had just carried out a commemorative group of buildings at Hiroshima that applied LeCorbusier's architectural principles on a civic scale, producing a creditable Corbusian urban ensemble before Corbu himself had an opportunity to do so at Chandigarh. (It may not be entirely ironic that a bomb-cleared site provided an ideal starting point for executing Corbusian conceptions.) At the same time, the cultural dependency of modern Japanese architecture was signaled by the visible role of Antonin Raymond, the European-American architect who was putting up office buildings and brutalist concrete churches in Tokyo that ranked with Tange's latest works as the inspiration of the next generation of Japanese architects.

For the Westerner visiting Japan in the 1950s the most profound lessons in architecture lay, of course, in its glorious architectural heritage—the Zen temples and gardens, the Shinto shrines, the surviving villas and palaces, and the pre-Meiji urban neighborhoods. And for me these remain achievements that no architect can hope to surpass.

The challenge of such ancient wonders to the development of an avant-garde is something we Americans do not have to face. We have had the ironic freedom of inventing new architectural form without such daunting relics in our midst: no Katsura Villa, no Ginkakuji temple, no Ise shrines (and, for that matter, no baroque churches or Mughal mosques).

My reaction to any new work in Japan is inevitably conditioned by these exemplars from the past. I look for signs of that peculiarly Japanese austerity, those subtle shifts in repetitive patterns, those contrasts of rich incident with sublime blankness. It is easy to find these beloved characteristics in much of the current Japanese work identified in this book as avant-garde—in the buildings of Fumihiko Maki or Tadao Ando, for example. It is harder for me to appreciate avant-garde work that rebels against these traditions—that is based almost entirely in Western tradition, as in the case of Isozaki's Tsukuba building, or defies just about all building tradition, as does the work of Shin Takamatsu. Intellectually, however, I can understand their urge to rebel—to defy everyone's expectations of Japanese architecture (even their own)—and to express the dynamism and conflict, the pain and disorder of life, as opposed to the traditional discretion and balance.

Rebellion as an option for the Japanese avant-garde is all the more understandable because the structure of the profession there deepens the division of architects between the two poles of establishment servant and outsider artist. To a much greater extent than in America or Western Europe, large-scale commercial and public building is assigned to huge design-build companies and big, service-oriented architecture firms. The individual design-oriented practitioners follow an alternative course and do so for life. There is virtually no chance that they would—as their U.S. counterparts might—take some business-minded partners or associates and build large firms of their own. Although these masters of design-oriented offices may work on some very large commissions, their permanent assignment to the more artistic side of a divided profession tends to nurture a more critical, more experimental point of view.

Another circumstance tending to institutionalize this artist-outsider position is the patchwork nature of the Japanese city (which is well portrayed in Hajime Yatsuka's essay and elsewhere in this book). Moderately large buildings that could stand out as landmarks in a Western city are largely enveloped in the visual disorder. (There is definitely economic and social order in these cities, but visually it is hard to detect.) The two Maki buildings described in this book illustrate the effect: His large and distinctive Spiral Building is swallowed up in the commercial turmoil of a Tokyo street, while his museum in Kyoto, at the entrance to a cultural precinct in this exceptional, grid-planned city, has the kind of urban prominence we expect in the West. Because so many of their works are hidden away in the prevailing urban hurly-burly or scattered in endless suburbs, the works of the artist architects tend to remain more limited in their public impact, more marginal except to initiates, than works of comparable scale in the West.

For the most part, today's Japanese avant-garde simply accepts this urban condition—even enjoys its chaotic energy. The architects represented in this book are not proposing alternative urban forms, as the metabolists did.

What today's avant-garde does offer, if at more modest scale, is brilliant experimentation in architecture, as such. There is probably no place on earth today more hospitable to this kind of built, inhabited speculation, and there are serious, often exhilarating, lessons in this book for all architects and architecture-lovers.

Stamford, Connecticut, 1990

ARCHAEOLOGY OF A FRAGMENTED LANDSCAPE: THE NEW AVANT-GARDE OF URBAN ARCHITECTURE IN JAPAN

Botond Bognar

The Japanese Progress

"The days when there was an immutable style...are past. ...The classical urban order having collapsed, any work of architecture that, in a sense, internalizes the city and functions on its exterior surface as a mechanism of [information] transmission will...symbolize today's image of the city—an environment that is fragmented but that constantly renews its vitality precisely through its state of fragmentation." Fumihiko Maki, "Spiral"[1]

FOLLOWING THE Meiji restoration in the mid–19th century, Japan opened its gates to the West and the rest of the world, signaling the end of more than 200 years of isolation in the Edo Era (1603–1868), and the beginning of its rapid modernization in the years to follow. It was clear to the Japanese that if they wanted to become a partner and eventually an equal member of Western so-ciety, they had to catch up with their Western counter-parts in nearly every respect. Japan lagged behind in the fields of social, political, industrial, and commercial de-velopments.[2] In addition, there was a serious lack of sci-entific and technological know-how. And so, just as they had borrowed from Chinese culture throughout a signif-icant period of their history, the Japanese now had to adopt elements of Western civilization. Once again, a massive and purposeful borrowing became a matter of survival; indeed Japan had to accomplish a lot in a very short period of time.[3]

Initially, contemporary Western architecture was introduced to Japan by invited foreign architects and educators.[4] By the turn of the century, however, the newly trained first generation of modern Japanese architects took the leading role in maintaining close contact with the new developments in European and American ar-chitecture. Several young Japanese designers went to work with architects such as Le Corbusier or Walter Gro-pius, to learn and eventually implement many of the ar-chitectural principles of the modern movement and the

Bauhaus in Japanese architecture.

The spread of the International Style, however, was soon to encounter strong resistance from, and later, explicit oppression by, the ruling military and government circles, who favored nationalistic architecture. Thus, while technological advancement and developments in engineering were pursued at an increasingly feverish pace, especially after the devastating 1923 Kanto earthquake, many of the new buildings were packaged in "a Japanese style founded in Oriental taste."[5] Western modern architecture was submerged until after Japan's defeat in World War II and the rebirth of the country as a new democratic society.

After the war, Japan underwent an unparalleled development and emerged as an industrial superpower and formidable rival of advanced Western societies. The principles of modern production and consumption—productivist rationalism, instrumental reason, universal technology, and utilitarianism—also gained further ground. The negative impact of all this progress, while mitigated by Japanese traditions and attitudes, was aggravated by the country's geographical conditions, its lack of available terrain, and high population density. Yielding to the economic boom, the explosive developments in industry, urbanization, and society, neither the land nor the urban environment could avoid the consequences of growing abuse and exploitation. In some instances, the face of the land has been scarred beyond recovery, while cities, seriously damaged by increasing pollution, congestion and land speculation, have become lesser places for human habitation. In most of these respects, too, Japan has caught up with, and even surpassed, its Western counterparts.

The Development and Present State of Urbanism

Although the important changes in architecture began around the second part of the 19th century when Japan was first exposed *en bloc* to modern, technologically advanced Western society and civilization, the urban fabric and the character of the Japanese city did not alter much on the whole until the beginning of the country's postwar reconstruction.[6] While the numerous cities devastated by the war were rebuilt along mainly traditional lines by their citizens, thus preserving previous urban "structural" characteristics, rapid social developments also made it necessary to provide for large-scale expansion along with more efficient urban planning.[7] The urban design principles of the modern movement were thus freely embraced. This resulted in an unprecedented urbanization; today, with more than 60% of its population of 120 million living in densely-built urban areas, Japan is one of the most urbanized of countries (1).

The fast-escalating "megalopolitan project," or "Japan-the-city," ushered in by contemporary industrial and consumer society and predicated on the productivist rationalism of modernist urbanism, began to open up the densely woven and ambiguous fabric of the traditional city. On the one hand, rigid and deterministic patterns emerged along with a growing number of autonomous buildings, epitomized by the popular high-rise, often along urban highways and expressways. On the other hand, the trivializing and irrational practices of consumerism have penetrated the urban realm so thoroughly and insidiously that practically every segment of the built environment and urban life has been converted into a form of commodity (2). Toyo Ito, one of the new generation architects, has written revealingly about the effects of megalopolitan development on the Japanese city: "Today Tokyo's old resilience is being covered up by a rigid frame. The city itself is gradually rigidifying. [Yet], while modernizing and becoming more and more controlled, Tokyo preserves, if only latently, a resilience and flexibility that accounted for its wonders and charm, that are not to be found in Western cities. How much longer it will be able to preserve these qualities is a moot point. The rigidifying process is proceeding every day. Afraid of it, people surround themselves with consumer code items in the form of decorations. And the heavier the ornament, the emptier."[8]

In the recent history of Japanese urbanism, there have been several attempts to rescue the city. The first was instigated in the early 1960s by Kenzo Tange and his disciples, who distanced themselves from the functionalist, urban model of the modern movement. The new and large-scale proposals for a metabolist architecture and urbanism were patterned along quasi-structuralist principles derived from Saussurian linguistics and the anthropology of Lévi-Strauss. Tange's famous Tokyo Plan (1960), as well as numerous other visionary or utopian projects by Kiyonori Kikutake, Kisho Kurokawa, and even Arata Isozaki, were all intended to afford greater flexibility than the modernist city (3, 4). They were also meant to avoid the pitfalls of the commodification of the urban realm by the increasing pull of the megalopolitan marketplace. The fast-developing, and by then readily available, industrial technology seemed to offer a direction to follow. Consequently, the new architectural and urban schemes, in which there was always a sharp distinction between interchangeable elements (a kind of capsule architecture) and permanent, built urban structures (mainly infrastructures), were propelled by a rather naive faith in industrial and technological progress as the answer to all the problems of urbanism, and even those of society itself (5). Yet, because they overemphasized industrialization and "structuration," the projects that were actually realized, including Tange's Osaka Expo (1970), turned out to be extremely heavy, inflexible, and over-deterministic with regard to their megastructures (6). In addition, despite the designers' intentions, the proposed changeability of the mass-produced and quickly obsolescent or outmoded architectural units began to play into the hands of a "metabolist consuming process," yielding to an implicitly consum-

1. *Densely built Ota Ward, Tokyo*

2. *Shibuya Station Square, Tokyo*

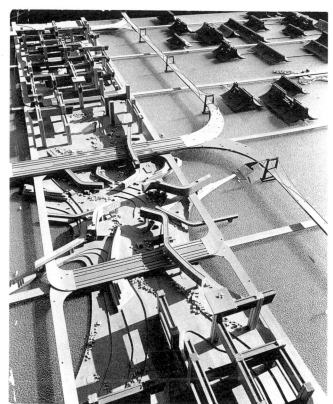

5. *Kisho Kurokawa, Nakagin Capsule Tower, Tokyo, 1972*

3. *Kenzo Tange, Tokyo Plan, 1960*

4. *Arata Isozaki, City in the Sky, 1962*

erist architecture.[9]

More sensitive and successful were Fumihiko Maki's attempts at reinterpreting a Japanese-type contextualism to cope with urban issues and create a more public architecture. Working from his notion of "group form," Maki aimed at a reciprocal relationship between urban elements and their organizing system, that is, between the parts and the whole.[10] Maki's healthy skepticism about a technological approach to urban and architectural design soon led him away from metabolist ideology and practice. He became interested in the ambiguous spatial relationships that could exist in, and generate, the "collective form" of the urban realm *(7)*. Eventually, however, he too had to realize that the public domain he intended to foster, as well as the entire urban context that he hoped to take into consideration, were being rapidly overrun by the megalopolitan project, whose imperatives for consumerist urbanism were systematically depriving every possible element in the city of its context. In this sense, the Japanese architect today has no choice but to add to the restless image of the city.

The Japanese urbanscape as it appears today would surely surpass any previous expectations of a first-time casual observer, not only with regard to the extreme density of the built urban fabric and the omnipresent crowd, but also in respect to the quality of the city as a human experience. This new environment is so extensive and overwhelming that any prior knowledge of Japan demands radical reinterpretation; indeed, everything related to Japan can only be understood against the background of the Japanese city. This phenomenon puts contemporary architectural intentions in a new light; the relationship between architecture and its urban context is one of the most important aspects of understanding both today's architecture and the city in Japan.

What are the qualities, then, that make the city appear so incomprehensible, at least to Westerners? The list of extremes starts with the immediately apparent: the radical heterogeneity of the constitutive elements that are, more often than not, and even overwhelmingly

in certain areas, non-architectural. To put it another way: alongside, over, and within architecture, one finds a forest of non-architectural elements so thick that it sometimes covers up or even replaces architecture entirely. If one were to characterize this encounter with the environment, one could do so by referring to the pervasiveness of signs, symbols, billboards, and supergraphics, as a kind of progressive anarchy. It seems Roland Barthes hit the mark when he called Japan the "Empire of Signs" *(8)*.[11]

While this is a striking phenomenon, there is a less visible aspect of the city which is more significant, notably the fact that these icons, just as much as every other element, fail to add up to something coherent or orderly, imparting instead a kind of visual uncertainty. There are no clear rational patterns with which to structure both perception and understanding of the physical urban environment as a totality. Nor is there a sense of a functioning and dominant center in this maze-like network of events. Every attempt to come to terms with its essence by way of rational cognition or logic fails; the puzzling and often theatrical insubstantiality of the Japanese city wins out, and a feeling of impermanence prevails. Tokyo reminds the Westerner that the rational is merely one system among others. As Barthes observed: "This city can be known only by an activity of an ethnographic kind: you must orient yourself in it not by book, by address, but by walking, by sight, by habit, by experience; here every discovery is intense and fragile, it can be repeated or recovered only by memory of the trace it has left in you."[12]

This quality of the contemporary Japanese city, however, is the result of several factors. Most importantly, it is as much the product of the development or progress of our post-industrial consumer society and its fast-escalating megalopolitan project as it is the outcome of the longstanding perceptive sensibilities of the Japanese manifested in their cultural, architectural, and urban traditions. Understanding the interrelationship and contradiction between these two factors is now seen by

6. *Kenzo Tange, Space Frame, Festival Plaza, Osaka Expo, 1970*

7. *Fumihiko Maki, Hillside Terrace Apartments, Tokyo, 1969–76*

8. *Shinjuku entertainment district, Tokyo*

Historic Background

While it is not obvious to the eyes of the short-term visitor, the evolution of today's "post-structuralist" city began, in fact, far back in the history of Japanese architecture and urbanism. A thorough investigation of the numerous surviving traditional architectural compounds and urban districts with regard to both their conception and perception reveals manifest signs of this origin, as well as a similarity between traditional forms of urbanism and certain recent urban design intentions of a new generation of architects.

The first permanent capitals in Japan were planned and laid out along the model of the Chinese city Chang'an, which had a rigid, geometrical gridiron pattern with major and minor roads running parallel in east-west and north-south directions, while the whole was surrounded by fortified city walls. Within this clearly delineated and homogenous urban system, significant buildings, including the Imperial Palace compound, held their well-defined location.[13] If we regard this Chinese model as the initial source or impetus, it might be said that the further evolution of Japanese urbanism was characterized by the growing deviation from this model. This deviation, which in fact bordered on a conscious act of violation, started with the fact that these early Japanese cities were not fully built as planned.[14]

Heian-kyo, or Kyoto, which succeeded the previous, short-term capitals in 794 A.D. and retained its status as such until the middle of the 19th century, not only increased in size and population, but also developed along new and increasingly haphazard patterns in response to topographical conditions, modes of life, and the Japanese mentality.[15] Subsequent rebuilding after numerous devastating fires provided the opportunities for these changes, often referred to as a process of Japanization *(9)*. Kyoto today has an urban structure that reveals both its original gridiron pattern and the random network of later streets "superimposed" over previous ones. In the absence of urban squares and piazzas, the extensive and

the new generation of architects as a key issue that guides their intentions in responding to present-day urban conditions of which they seem to be acutely aware.

9. *Kyoto as planned and as developed until 19th century*

1. Imperial Palace compound
2. Suzaku-mon Gate
3. Higashi Sanjo Mansion
4. West Market
5. East Market
6. Suzaku Avenue
7. Toji Temple
8. Kinkaku-ji Temple
9. Daitoku-ji Monastery
10. Shimogamo Shrine
11. Ginkaku-ji Temple
12. Kamo River
13. Nanzen-ji Temple
14. Koymizu-dera Temple

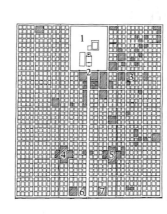

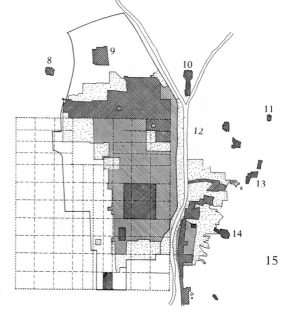

15

intricate network of streets and street-architecture came to provide the public space where city life and communal activities took place.

Equally complex patterns of streets structured the development of many other kinds of urban settlements as well, in which, from the very beginning, rectangular grids played only a limited role, or no role at all. Among these were the castle towns which, from the 16th century on, were to become important centers of the country's political, economic, and social life, gradually forming the urban cores for most of Japan's modern cities. In castle towns, for defense purposes, main roads and thoroughfares were laid out with numerous bends and ran only through the merchants' quarters, never the center. Tokaidō, for example, the famous highway between Edo (Tokyo) and Kyoto, bent 27 times while crossing the town of Okazaki. In addition, there were practically no cross-streets; the majority of intersections were T- or L-shaped.

This kind of arrangement of streets, in addition to the quality of Japanese architecture, is vital not only in bringing about a unique layering of urban space, but also in defining separate urban zones or districts, often distinguished and identified by the activities of the artisans who lived and worked there. As particular trades were assigned to certain locations, it was not unusual for these places to carry particular names such as the salt-sellers' district, carpenters' district, or metalworkers' district, as in the case of Kanazawa. Even today, specific shops, cinemas, theaters, and other cultural institutions or entertainment complexes can be found grouped in distinct areas that are customarily not part of the city core or center. Thus, while the irregular but sensitive texture or "sophisticated order" of the traditional townscape has prevailed in most instances, even if only latently, the eventual demolition of many castles and the growing influence of commercial and other developments have gradually increased the process of urban fragmentation.[16] William Coaldrake observed that Tokyo, one such previous castle town, "spread as the sum of its parts, not as a measured whole."[17]

This phenomenon is further reinforced by the traditionally weak or ambiguous character of urban centers. In its layout, the Chinese city, a prototype for early Japanese capitals, did not have a center, and this quality was to prevail with a special emphasis in Japan. The Imperial Palace compound within the homogeneous grid was located at the northern end of the north-south axis and, as a walled-in area and "forbidden city," it was, and still is, off limits to the general public. Even the other types of consecutive settlements lacked the large and open city squares or plazas defined by a concentration of public buildings and institutions which could provide a political and spiritual core and dominant center for the city.

In Japanese cities, important buildings were lined along streets and spaced at certain intervals.[18] Religious compounds were often located along the perimeter or outside the city. Medieval castle towns, having no city walls, assigned numerous temples to the outskirts for defensive purposes. Yet, while the town had no special or well-defined boundaries, such as defensible walls, but only soft layers of buildings and other wooden structures, often merely as signs like the torii gate, the castle compound itself was surrounded by layers of both strong stone walls and moats. Thus the dominant, central part, similar to the Imperial Palace compound, was again enclosed and forbidden to most citizens. Today in Tokyo, where the residence of the emperor is located in the innermost precinct of the remaining Edo castle, the original center of the city is an unattainable, invisible, closed area. Such features prompted Terunobu Fujimori to compare Japanese cities to cabbages, wrapped in soft, protective layers, and Western cities to eggs, encased in hard shells.[19] To further clarify the underlying issues, Shuji Takashina aptly pointed out that "whereas Westerners tend to view space in a unified and convergent manner, that is, in terms of a discrete, organized whole, the Japanese see it in a pluralistic, divergent manner, in terms of numerous interconnecting fragments."[20]

The evolution of the urban environment in Japan indicates that the city is created, perceived, and understood as an additive texture (text?) wherein preference is given to the parts (or episodes) in a network of independent places; the whole (or the story) as an aggregate or incomplete form, remains elusive, to be conjured up only in the memory and imagination of the perceiver. As typified best by Tokyo, the Japanese city has neither the structural clarity of European cities, nor the geometric gridiron pattern of American cities. Instead, it has grown up in a pleat-like, irregular way around a number of nuclei or, as Vladimir Krstic remarked, "it has developed with no apparent concept of its totality."[21]

In addition, urban buildings in densely built rows and the streets they faced were customarily mediated, as well as defined, by the sometimes extensive yet refined application of Japanese signs and symbols which, being regularly changed either by necessity or consensus, never added up to a definitive or rigid order (10). And, as the buildings were usually made of thin, light, and perishable materials, they too were often changed, rebuilt, or relocated. The ritual of periodic rebuilding of Shinto shrines is a case in point, although ordinary buildings also had to be repeatedly reconstructed because their wood and paper structures were easily and frequently destroyed in the numerous wars, earthquakes, and fires, that have plagued Japan throughout its history.[22] Thus, those buildings also tended to acquire a character similar to shrines, pagodas, and others that were important symbols and/ or signs. And so, the Japanese city as an interpretative labyrinth has come to be denoted, to a surprising extent, by the display of signs and symbols rather than by the physical and permanent entity of its objects or enclosures. Indeed, as has been said, the Japanese "do not comprehend urban space" as Americans and Europeans do, through a grid pattern or a radiating network, "but rather through collage or the empirical composition of

16

10. *Traditional urban row houses, Gion Corner, Kyoto*

symbols discontinuously scattered about.''[23] These qualities, which impart a feeling of insubstantiality and impermanence, as well as of the mutability of human life, or of existence and meaning in general, indicate the implicit but significant influence of the Oriental world views of Shintoism, Buddhism, etc., on the urban environment, rendering the city as stage and manifest part of the "floating world" of the Japanese.[24]

The Consumerist Urban Desert

There is no doubt that much of what makes Tokyo and other Japanese cities so kaleidoscopic today finds its origin in the historic development of Japanese urbanism. Yet, despite their apparent similarities, there exist significant, even if not immediately obvious, differences between the premodern or Edo Period and contemporary, consumerist urban tendencies in Japan.

The former created a largely indeterminate environment with a sophisticated order whose perception had to involve both active physical participation and imaginative interpretation. In such a perception of (urban) reality—similar to the Buddhist conduct of critical self-awareness leading or alluding to a non-rational "plural void" (*mu*)—the perceiving subject and the perceived

world could be both identical and different at the same time, while the meaning of the built environment could afford to be neither absolute nor relative. Today, however, we live in and foster an urban nexus in which systems of signs and symbols are being reduced to their pure instrumentality in order to be turned into advertisements and other forms of consumer persuasion or propaganda; they are predetermined by the ultimate purpose of consumption. This process is supported by the pervasive apparatus of mass-media which, together with the homogeneity of a consumer-oriented society, as Krstic points out, "creates a milieu highly conducive to the imposition and manipulation of unified value and preference systems in all aspects of social life."[25] Promoting consumption can only be maintained if the urban environment, with regard to its form and created atmosphere, is conceived with a finiteness and instantaneousness of meaning in space; in fact, it is produced with a targeted accuracy.[26]

With the whole built environment rapidly turning into commodity, the flood of stimuli may parade under the banner of meaning, but actually such sensory overkill devalues everything, exploits symbols and other modes of communication, rendering the city increasingly meaningless. Today the Japanese city, as Ito observed, can no longer provide an oasis, only the growing devastation and

17

uniformity of the desert.[27] While these tendencies of the megalopolis are symptomatic of urbanism in capitalist societies in general, they are especially extreme in Japan, where certain surviving traditional modes of urbanism and socio-cultural features are particularly vulnerable, if not conducive, to consumerist exploitation. Yet, no one is more conscious of this urban predicament than the "unhappy" avant-garde of contemporary Japanese architects who, unavoidably, have to encounter the far-reaching consequences and ultimately closed-circuit limitations of the megalopolis on their designs.[28]

Following the bankruptcy of metabolist ideology in Japan, the past fifteen years have seen architects react in a wide variety of ways to the developing, but also deteriorating, urban conditions. There is, however, one common aspect: it has become clear to everyone that the age of large-scale, revolutionary urban schemes, based on a technocratic utopianism, is over. Such schemes would not only be highly questionable, but also impossible within the current social, ideological, and cultural climate of the new *fin-de-siècle*; and in this respect the city is not regarded as being subject to design. By the early 1970s the avant-garde of Japanese architecture was overrun by the very progress of modernism, or the megalopolitan project that modern architects, including the metabolists, had been so eager to foster. Having lost its *raison d'être*, avant-gardism now is giving way to a new, late avant-gardism or an *arrière-garde*, to use Kenneth Frampton's term, which, instead of unequivocally promoting progress, attempts both to question and resist its myth and demagogic tendencies.[29] The need for, and nature of, such resistance, however, is not always recognized or understood equally by everyone.

An Architecture of Resistance

Since the early 1970s, a large number of architects searching for replacements for lost universal symbols have indulged in what is generally known as the language game; they still believe in the possibility of establishing identity in "the city without quality." So desperate are they to invent new styles, forms, and meanings to make their own personal trademarks, they do not always realize that in fact they only add to the urban Babel. Yet, as Hajime Yatsuka points out, "the tragedy is not necessarily in their beliefs but in the semantic universe which surrounds them."[30] The megalopolitan marketplace is restless and anxious to gobble up all things, especially easily identifiable styles and products in order to convert them into marketable images. In so doing, it devalues them at an astonishing pace. Scores of designers have fallen prey to this process, many not surviving or recovering from losing the game, in what Chris Fawcett so aptly called "a kind of aesthetic Russian roulette".[31]

Those who were less convinced about a formalistic contextual approach to urbanism had other options open to them. While the game prevailed, now the intention of the so-called new wave of Japanese architecture was to transform the rules of the game.[32] The first sign of this was the designing of an increasing number of buildings that represented a deliberate retreat from the city. Many architects felt that under the given conditions, the traditionally conciliatory relationship between building and the city, or between the private and public realms, was difficult if not impossible to maintain. The resulting introverted and defensive architecture was meant to be a bulwark of resistance. In order to protect the inhabitants from the growing hazards of the urban environment, designers frequently opted to seal off hermetically the interior from the exterior. While there was little communication between inside and out, the small inner world, or hermetic microcosm, concealed in solid concrete buildings with a hard-surfaced geometry was to provide the conditions for moments of silence in which the individual could recreate himself physically and spiritually.[33]

These buildings, usually small houses, either showed only a blank face or simply turned their backs to the city in a manner that was explicitly anti-urban or indifferent at best. Yet, inside they all attempted to evoke a new human reality and self-awareness, often by consciously challenging if not provoking customary perceptions and habitual associations. In other words, new relations between the space and the person were intended to engender new modes and meanings of existence. Thus Tadao Ando's minimalist architecture of austere simplicity reinterpreted the calmness of traditional *sukiya*-style architecture and the courtyard arrangement of the urban residence or *machiya*, and in so doing also expressed a manifest criticism of the hedonistic and conformist tendencies of contemporary bourgeois society in both architecture and urbanism *(11, 34)*. Ando has written: "My approach is to pursue more than superficial comfort. I want to try to recapture one by one the truly enduring and essential elements of the human residence, many of which have been abandoned in the course of rapid economic growth: basic relations with nature, direct dialogue with materials, the small discoveries and surprises people can detonate in their daily life-spaces, the pleasure and aesthetic uplift to be had from creative initiative in a simple way of life".[34]

Kazuo Shinohara, Toyo Ito, and even Hiroshi Hara followed a similar line in the early 1970s. Their buildings also rejected the amorphous urban environment.[35] Consider, for example, Shinohara's small residential buildings, such as the House in Uehara (1976) and the House at a Curved Road (1978), or Ito's U-House in Nakano (1976), all of which appear as discontinuous, alienated objects in the urban context of Tokyo. The experience inside them, however, eludes definition or objective description, suspending spatial reality and the rational awareness of the mind. The space in the U-House formed by two white, smoothly curving parallel concrete walls has no visible center, no clear direction, and no end. Nothing is fixed, nothing is absolute. The light penetrat-

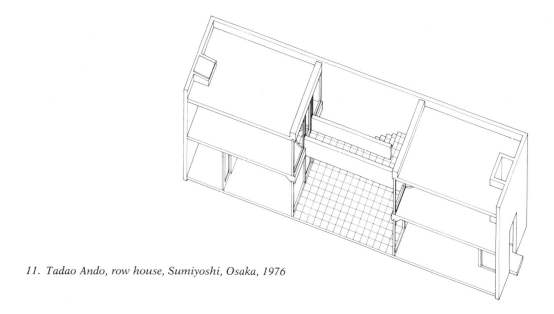

11. *Tadao Ando, row house, Sumiyoshi, Osaka, 1976*

12. *Toyo Ito, U-House, Nakano, Tokyo, 1976*

ing a slot in the slanting roof and the one and only window to the empty courtyard—the negative center—destabilizes the usual reference system of our perception. The soft light bouncing off the surfaces washes the interior into immaterial existence. The feeling is like being in a dark cave or inside the womb *(12, 36)*.

It has to be pointed out, however, that no matter how much these buildings appear to be anti-urban, they are not necessarily against the city. As Hara explained, they only express "a critical attitude toward the present-day urban communities."[36] Indeed, a closer investigation reveals that many examples of this defensive architecture, including Hara's own "reflection houses," strive to recreate "another city" within the realm of these individual buildings. Hara has designed many houses with a sequence of centrally-located spaces as "public" domains, such as "urban" streets or stairways lined with miniature and metaphoric urban fragments: plazas, landmarks, intersections, and the façades of the inward-looking rooms, all under the skylights of the whole house *(13)*. Ando, too, has designed most of his small buildings with tiny open-air courtyards as "urban squares" complete with bridges and stairs. A similar intention is evident in the "fissure spaces" within Shinohara's Incomplete (1970), and Repeating Crevice (1972) Houses in Tokyo, not to mention many of Isozaki's larger-scale public buildings, such as the Gunma and Kitakyushu Museums (1975) or Kamioka City Hall (1978) *(14)*.

What is represented in these designs is a curious inversion of urbanism in which paradoxical models of the city are recreated within autonomous buildings. Hara wrote about his intention to "bury the trove of the city within the house," while Ito acknowledged creating "small-scale Utopias" within enclosed buildings.[37] Nevertheless, these remarks, as much as the buildings themselves, also highlight the dilemma and frustration

19

13. Hiroshi Hara, Hara House, Machida, 1974

14. Arata Isozaki, Gunma Museum, Takasaki, 1974

faced by those who, in reaction to the increasingly meaningless external world and contemporary life, try to find a more liberating, though private and autonomous order in which to live. Their attempts inevitably result in isolation and lose the possibility for a common ground within the public realm in which meaning is ultimately rooted. The dilemma is that while the megalopolis effectively prevents public discourse in the city, the operation and effects of the mass media are impossible to keep out completely, even by hermetic concrete enclosures.

The Changing Course of Design

As it has become more conscious about the impossibility of such a state of affairs, the avant-garde of Japanese architects has begun to shift direction and rearrange strategies. The defensive attitude and retreat from the urban realm have been replaced by a willingness to confront the megalopolis on its own terms. Now, there is not only a reinterpretation of the notion of "burying the city within architecture," but also an increased interest in "embedding architecture in the city."[38] This means that much of the new architecture is becoming simultaneously both continuous and discontinuous with the Japanese city while, at its best, not relinquishing its critical stance. The previous attitude of violence and radical confrontation has been tamed into more poetic and, perhaps, more effectively critical modes of design, alluding to the notion of *le poétique*.[39]

The latently preserved flexibility, vital energy, dynamics, and resilience of the Japanese city are being rediscovered in a new renaissance of urbanism in Japan. Architects have started to respond to the city with new and heightened sensibilities. The paradox is that architecture now not only exposes the increasingly elusive forces of the megalopolis, but is also often turned into both a weapon and a shield against them. For example, Shinohara's House Under High Voltage Lines (1981) in Tokyo, could, as Marc Treib observed, be read as both "an act of obeisance in which the roof plane has bowed to the invisible powers of public utilities . . . [and also] as an act of defiance in which architecture does not retreat, but presses its face against the unseen force—though deformed by it in the process."[40]

In other words, these works of the avant-garde are characterized by an inherent ambiguity: they are both an assimilation of, and contrast to, the city, and accordingly, the boundaries within them between creative (poetic) and critical processes are also dissolved. If architects previously wanted to bend the rules of the language game, now they attempt to break them, to question the whole game altogether with the aim of opening up the closed and reductivist circuits of signification or Western representation. Instead of searching for a defining context, designers are shifting their attention to a more liberating indefinite textuality of the built environment; the city is understood as an open text within the discursive

practices of society. As is obvious, these intentions also reflect many aspects of contemporary Western philosophy, including post-structuralism, and deconstructionist criticism.

More precisely, the goal is to seek out gaps in the rules of the form-creating and meaning-generating game, and then, through these uncovered interstices, dismantle or critically deconstruct its system and internal logic. In this way both form and meaning are prevented from appearing as self-evident, natural (or ahistorical), and finished entities, and so, are less open to objectification and exploitation by the market place. In such an integration without synthesis, totality cannot be and is not presented in a state of visual completeness or perfection; the whole has to be repeatedly reconstituted with the help of memory and imagination. A fragmentary integration destabilizes the fixed, one-point perspective or naturalized perception; it demands that the observer acquire a multifocal perspective in order to interpret and intuitively understand the reality of this architecture, which elicits a mutual, and perhaps also critical, engagement between the interpreting subject and the interpreted object, tying the person into the world by a multitude of invisible threads. Objects tend to suspend their objective character while subjects are prompted to relinquish their subjectivity and lose their independence and opposition. Here, neither the created world nor human beings can claim self-contained and delimited autonomy.

In this architecture, totality is unstable, fragile, and threatened by imminent disintegration. Thus, many new buildings in Japan remind us of the poignancy of things on the verge of disappearing or, conversely, on the point of emerging. Experiencing them is a process of suspending architecture in a perpetually evanescent and temporary state of "in-between" where becoming and fading away, growth and decay, presence and absence, reality and fiction, silence and speech take place simultaneously—or perhaps are one and the same thing. It is in this sense that many of these designs evoke the images of elusive phenomena, of twilight, shadows, clouds, or mirage, and gain a certain ephemeral or fictive quality.

It is important to point out, however, that deconstructing form and meaning, i.e., the language of architecture and urbanism itself, does not, and should not, mean their complete elimination or destruction. It does not mean, as in populist and reactionary postmodernism, that all positions are now open or that "anything goes." Rather it acknowledges a critical path of practice that destructures form and meaning in order to reinscribe them in a significantly different way, a way that frees us from the authority of literal facts while denying the idea of a privileged mode of representation within a privileged aesthetic realm, and under the rule of a privileged "center." The aim is to restore and play out differences, without opposition, by way of a critical mediation that goes beyond the strict dualism of objectivism and relativism and attempts to achieve a "structure of difference" or "order of chaos." In Japan, it appears as no accident that this new, non-Western mode of understanding and conduct echoes many aspects of the traditional Japanese mentality also expressed in the legacies of the historic city.

Architecture, the City and Nature

Gaps within present day received, predictable conditions are sought along new sensibilities informed by both a heightened or vibrant anxiety and laconic stoicism that characterize equally the new *fin-de-siècle* cultural and intellectual climate and the architectural and urban landscape in Japan. The rediscovery and reinterpretation of nature's intimate relation to architecture is one such gap through which architects are escaping the urban and cultural predicament of today. Recent works by Hara, Yamamoto, Ito, Hasegawa, not to mention Ando, all make various comments about nature by way of, and in relation to, architecture.

Building upon his understanding of the opposition between culture and nature, Tadao Ando sets nature against the trivializing tendencies of both contemporary mass culture and the megalopolis. However, he generally excludes vegetation from his work, an act which, as Frampton points out, "stems from a realization that planting is invariably employed today as a cheap ameliorative device; that is to say, as a sentimental aestheticization of an otherwise sterile, if not brutal, condition."[41] Today even nature has fallen victim of commodification (think of the excessive amount of greenery put in planters, with the calculated simulation of a natural atmosphere, inside shopping malls and commercial centers). For Ando, therefore, nature is signified as void rather than represented by naturalized images of nature.

In order to avoid the reduction of his buildings to consumable images, Ando works toward an architecture based on experience rather than appearance. The essence of his works is a paradox insofar as they are designed with the purpose of creating substantial voids that can reject every absolute, including the notion of center. The courtyards found in all of his works, even the smallest houses, introduce nature's evocative and provocative power in the form of wind, rain, snow, and the "framed sky"—the shapeless, formless, and as such, not easily reducible manifestations of our natural world, which, when directly exposed to the realm of habitation, are capable of continuously challenging our utilitarian and materialistic aspirations. Ando's nature sneaks into his buildings and gains meaning through the gap that exists or that he purposely opens between function and architecture.

Ando writes: "The aim of my design is to impart rich meaning to spaces through natural elements and the many aspects of daily life. Such things as light and wind only have meaning when they are introduced inside the house in a form cut off from the outside world. The isolated fragments of light and air [can] suggest the entire natural world" (15).[42] This attitude, not unlike the one in which Japanese *haiku* is conceived, is as poetically inspired as it is also critical of the superficiality and increasing conformity of contemporary life-styles.

15. *Tadao Ando, Koshino House, Ashiya, 1982*

This peculiar paradox, whereby the totality of nature is fragmented in order to retain its entirety, is still evident in Ando's designs of the mid–1980s. The Time's Building (1984), the Rokko Chapel (1985), or the "Jun" Port-Island Building (1985), however, have more generous sites than their predecessors in the 1970s and so respond more positively to the surrounding landscape or urbanscape (16). Yet, while his architecture is becoming unquestionably more open, and perhaps, less provocative than before, Ando continues to filter both nature and the city as he introduces them into his buildings. By way of layered walls and their interstices, partial enclosures and carefully focused openings—Ando's most important design interventions—nature and the site are transformed or architecturalized to lose their naturalized appearance; at the same time his architecture is turned into a porous matrix of indefinite spaces.

16. Tadao Ando, Rokko Chapel, Mt. Rokko, Kobe, 1986

Ando, however, is not alone in employing multi-layered walls to transform the conditions in which his buildings find themselves. When circumstances warrant, other architects, too, find this method rather beneficial. Thus, while Kunihiko Hayakawa's architecture encompasses a wide range of design approaches, in his three houses in Seijo (1982–88)—all facing a busy urban road with an intersection—he has successfully turned to the protective potentials of such arrangement. With multiple layers of concrete walls, limited openings and in-between zones, he provides a transition between the public urban and private residential realms, a boundary which is closed-yet-open.

Although Hiromi Fujii's concerns with "architectural metamorphology, deconstruction, de-composition, or desemiotization," and "the negativity of materialism" are basically different from those of Ando, his works, especially the more recent ones, also express a breaking down of the object of architecture.[43] If Ando is an architect of Heideggerean nearness, Fujii is of a critical distance as advocated by Theodor Adorno. Suspending form and meaning acquired through routine and naturalized perception has long been Fujii's preoccupation. His aim is to achieve a primordial state of man in which refer-

ences to everyday life are carefully bleached out in order to provoke a purely existential relationship between subject and object. Fujii reaches this state by way of a hyper-rational application of geometry that subjects architecture to a controlled accident. In his Shibaura Gym and Ushimado projects (both of 1985), every architectural proposition—walls, openings, spaces—is consistently transformed, reversed in a repetitive way. Architecture, as at Ushimado, gradually erodes into the breathtaking though hardly describable transcendental realm of the terrace.

The projects Mizoe no. 1 and no. 2 are the most recent attempts by Fujii to challenge the (architectural) world of classicism together with its unifying viewpoint, and supplant them with dispersed, multi-layered spaces with no one-point perspective. These projects are the first where he has introduced his full-fledged operations in strictly residential buildings; both the Mizoe no. 1 and no. 2 are model houses in Iizuka city on Kyushu Island. Moreover, the second project, as opposed to the still rectangular system of the first, is now the outcome of not only fragmented but also scattered walls and grids. Comprehending the spatial disposition in this case demands most obviously a continuously shifting viewpoint *(17)*.

23

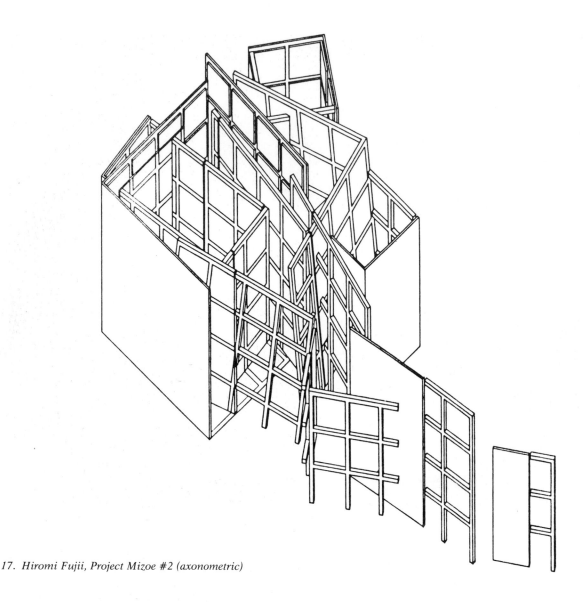

17. *Hiromi Fujii, Project Mizoe #2 (axonometric)*

Fujii writes: "In contemplating both the world of classicism and reality with all its variety and complexity, I am forced to consider the diverse visions that the latter affords.... The viewing subject, which we once regarded as a mirror reflecting immutable images, possesses distortions, like language, and is [but] a part of that [external] world as well."[44] Fujii's non-classical architecture, as exemplified best by both the Ushimado Building—a curious metaphor of a violated or disordered and ruinous Acropolis—and the Mizoe no. 1, thus is also a manifest criticism of today's urban architecture and its simplistic order of representation.

If one of Ando's intentions in design is to rediscover and reintroduce the unpredictable and changing phenomena of nature, Hara's new architectural concept of modality that aims at blurring the boundaries between nature and architecture displays a certain affinity with this intention.[45] In his recent buildings, especially the Tasaki Museum (1986), the Yamato International (1987),

and Iida City Museum (1988), architecture itself is articulated to approximate the quality of some natural phenomenon such as clouds, mist, rainbow, or mirage. *(18)*. The boundaries of these buildings are defined as vaguely as is possible in a built, multi-story structure. The undulating and fragmented volumes wrapped in reflective aluminum panels, the numerous, carefully patterned frosted-glass window panes, and the intricate system of paths traversing the spaces inside and out bring forth a multi-layered architecture. This is intended to relate to both the amorphous and ephemeral formations of nature and the structures of human consciousness that penetrate such phenomena. Hara's architecture of modality is thus in tune with nature as it is capable of "changing with the change of nature itself," while also being an attempt, like Marcel Duchamp's work, to "peep into consciousness."[46] Hara is trying to enact and grasp, through various scenes, his intuitive understanding of the idea that architecture, nature, and human consciousness

18. *Hiroshi Hara, Tasaki Museum, Karuizawa, 1986*

19. *Itsuko Hasegawa, House in Nerima, Tokyo, 1986*

are as inseparably interlaced as they are profoundly implicated in one another; their actual borders lie beyond their physical realm and, just as their forms, meanings and very nature, they are profoundly ambiguous.

Are not Takefumi Aida's recent explorations with architectural fluctuation, fragmentation, and scattering of three-dimensionality a move in the same direction? Leaving behind his toy-block houses, Aida has started to design primarily with two-dimensional, layered walls in parallel but non-compositional configurations that, in a curious manner, can endow his buildings with depth. A similar effect can be experienced looking upon the urban landscape: as if through a high-powered telescopic lens, the buildings seem to pile up and fluctuate. In this continuous flux, boundaries between architecture, the city, and nature are perceived as indeterminate.[47] In Aida's most successful work, such as the Kazama House (1987) and the Tokyo War Memorial Park (1988), the parallel, reinforced concrete walls effectively penetrate the entire realm of architecture and are able to loosen the constraints of closed, three-dimensional volumes into a more fluid spatial entity. When the "random" wall openings visually overlap, they focus on various events both inside

and out, filtering and blending interior and exterior worlds in a fragmented, yet highly poetic way.

The architecturalization of nature is also an aspect of the later works of both Ito and Hasegawa. Their buildings of thin, light-weight materials not only evoke, especially in Hasegawa's case, the forms of nature, but are also penetrated by natural elements, alluding to a condition in which architecture is created by, yet also dissolved in nature. This allusion to nature, however, has nothing to do with any sentimental recollection, or with yielding to the "fatal pull of the nostalgic." By the special application of industrially-produced elements, metallic screens, and soft fabric, nature is approached not simply as an idealized world offering escape from the harsh realities of present-day human and urban conditions, but rather as an ally with which to reveal and confront these conditions. Hasegawa writes: "I architecturalize images of nature because I want to express a view of the contemporary world—one that sees potential for living in greater freedom. I use architectural and technological details to evoke nature, and natural and cosmic details to evoke architecture" *(19, 40)*.[48]

In an attempt to address the urban problems posed

25

20. *Yasumitsu Matsunaga, Daita Housing Project, Tokyo, 1989*

by the radical transformation of the city in Japan, Matsunaga also explores not only the architecturalization of nature, but also that of cosmos. He wants to achieve this by way of a new epistemology, derivative of the tremendous advancement of frontier science which, as he sees it, "is almost approaching the sphere of transcendental thinking" while fusing the logic of physics with the intuitive insight of metaphysics.[49] He points out that, "if the picture of the world, in the eyes of the most advanced science, has been transformed drastically from what it used to be like, then architecture, which is supposed to reflect the world, could not escape a serious transition either."[50] He seems to be saying that architecture is still a model of the universe, but since our cosmic model of the world and nature has changed profoundly, the definition of architecture needs a serious reexamination today. His recent work of small houses, then, is propelled by an intention to establish a new paradigm of architecture which is apparently comparable to Abbé Laugier's prototypical primitive hut, except for the fact that in Matsunaga's case, nature as reference is supplanted by the man-made nature of our contemporary world of science, technology, and urbanization. In this sense Matsunaga's houses, particularly the Daita Housing Project (1989), reveal a certain affinity with Ito's vision of urban

nomad communities, while with regard to architecture's legitimation through cosmology or metaphysics the two architects follow basically different directions *(20, 41)*.

From these architectural intentions a new approach emerges that interprets the relation of the city and nature in an unorthodox manner, in which the city itself is often understood as nature. Beyond looking at the urban realm as merely an arena of economic, social, and political developments and/or conflicts, many Japanese architects (as well as writers and artists) have begun to see the city as a fertile land whose "life-pulse, chaotic energy, flux of desires, ways and means of perception—the alogic immanent in the urban nexus as Deleuzian *machine* or *corps sans organes*," can provide them with a multiplicity of impulses and incentives that other media cannot, fostering what may be called a city sensitivity.[51] Fumihiko Maki writes: "We receive certain messages out of the city which is almost like nature ... [thus] we take the city as a kind of man-made nature and try to respond to it."[52]

These responses manifest, nevertheless, a broad spectrum ranging between two distinct, even opposite tendencies. Whereas at one end of the spectrum we find the move toward the architecturalization of nature, at the other it is toward the naturalization of architecture. The first implies that nature is always subject to human interpretations and transformations, almost to the extent that *its* very nature appears unnatural, that is to say, it is also a historical construct; while the second approaches architecture as a natural phenomenon and thus maintains that its nature lies beyond history, or that it is ahistorical. The first position is best represented perhaps by Ito, the second by Hara, with the others taking various in-between positions, in this way blending the opposites along different emphases.

The City as Topography

Riken Yamamoto's recent buildings such as the Gazebo (1986), Rotunda (1987), and Hamlet (1988), share some of the intentions and characteristics of Ito's designs; they are covered by extensive tent-like structures to envelope spacious realms that are open to the changing conditions of climate and nature. However, unlike Ito's, Yamamoto's ambiguously defined realms, which are, in fact, the owners' residences, are elevated above their respective buildings; they sit atop a structure with which they do not seem to have any relationship other than that which architecture has with the soil in which it is grounded. Indeed, these substructures appear to have been constructed solely for the purpose of providing a base for the residences in the air, the only place where dwelling and "architecture" could still be assured and nourished over the unfriendly surface of the city *(21, 42)*.

As they fill gaps in the city, the lower sections of Yamamoto's buildings maintain, though not necessarily endorse, the continuity of the existing, disordered urban fabric, which manifests itself to him as something like a ragged, uneven substratum, or a fractal landscape. Yamamoto has spoken of the city as topography and, as such, part of a new nature.[53] The city as nature again? Perhaps, insofar as man-made landscapes of the past, like ruinous remains of ancient civilizations buried in the ground, can be interpreted as a time-conceived artificial nature or *topos*. This understanding of the existing city as having the quality of ruins recalls in some respects Isozaki's visionary Cities in the Sky, and the idea that every city in the future is increasingly bound to be built on the ruins of a present one.

Yamamoto, in his city-as-topography, not only implicitly acknowledges the fragmented nature of the Japanese urbanscape, but, while building upon the sedimentary and cumulative layers of this artificial site, tries to unearth much of its discovered "remains." Thus, his design process (and that of several other architects with a similar understanding) could be likened to the combined activities of a miner, an archaeologist, and a builder who, in a curious manner, dig out and use these resources *not* for the purpose of reconstructing the past, but for shaping the present and, *more so*, the future. Similarly, Ryoji Suzuki's Edge Building (1987) is an agglomeration of excavated fragments, or fossil specimens as he

21. *Riken Yamamoto, Gazebo, Yokohama, 1986*

calls them, which have been buried deep in the collective memory of the city and its inhabitants.[54] Above these fragments rearranged as new land, the owner's residence is located once again.

Hara's research into vernacular villages in the "primitive" cultures of Africa and Asia has had a steady influence in his designs even after they began to change and open more toward the surrounding natural and urban landscape. But, whereas previously he internalized the urban landscape, creating topological interior spaces, now he seems to turn this model inside out, making his new buildings metaphors of a city within the city. Thus, the Yamato International (1987), for example, appears as an inverted, though also exploded, version of a "reflection house," particularly of his own residence of 1974 *(13, 33)*. Yet the Yamato is placed not simply within the city, but also above it. The extensive, rigidly shaped base, which complies with the scale of the surrounding urban environment and the adjacent elevated highway, is but an artificial platform or *topos* on which a fictive vernacular village—Hara's new, shiny and fragmented urban construct—looms like an elusive mirage or, in Hiroshi Watanabe's words, "a high-tech Shangri-la."[55] It appears as if another of Isozaki's Cities in the Sky has landed here, though not quite: the Yamato is both continuous and discontinuous with the city on the ground.

27

The small belvedere with the moon-viewing platform on top of Hasegawa's House in Nerima, and the upper sections, the so-called acropolis of Maki's Spiral Building, express a similar vision, as does Shinohara's TIT Centennial Hall (1987), which could also be seen as a curious reinterpretation of the City in the Sky, in which the form and, perhaps, also the idea, are deliberately broken. Isozaki's "flying tube"—the actualized version of his visionary cities, implemented in the Oita Medical Hall (1960), Kitakyushu Museum (1975) and, in a certain sense, in the vaulted shapes of the Fujimi Country Club (1974)—reappears in the TIT building almost literally by accident. The flying half-cylindrical vault has landed on its back, with the impact breaking its volume and axis in the middle.

In all of these projects architecture is interpreted and shaped to mediate between various, often opposing phenomena: city and private habitat, land and sky, the man-made and the natural, order and disorder, the old and the new. This is done in a manner wherein a lower substructure, as part of an urban topography, upholds a superstructure with which it has only an accidental relationship. While this generally holds true, the actual realization of the idea displays a considerable variety of architectural articulation, among which the recollection of constructivism, even if often in the form of de-constructionism, emerges as the most conspicuous. The works of Yamamoto and Shinohara are good examples of this; in addition, Minoru Takeyama's new projects seem to point in the same direction.

Takeyama, who began his design career as a semiotician in the early 1970s with such "pop" buildings as the Ichiban-kan (1969) and Niban-kan (1970), has recently shifted the focus of his interest toward a quasi-constructivist architecture, while not necessarily abandoning the significant aspects of the language of architecture (22). His latest buildings, including the Tokyo Port Terminal Building to be completed in 1991, feature an impressive array of exposed structural elements and industrial materials, such as steel frames and surfaces. Built on newly reclaimed land—another kind of urban or artificial topography—in the Tokyo bay, the Port Terminal, like the works of Yamamoto, Hara, and Hasegawa, also represents an architecture of in-between. On the margins of sea and land, city and nature, this transparent/translucent construct of steel and glass, light and movement, of stairways, passages, and bridges, as well as of both high-tech and ordinary structure, aspires to a mode of building that is as poetic as it is critical; it seems to mediate among the conflicting urban, industrial landscape and seascape as much as it also holds them at bay.

The City of Urban Nomads

It is obvious that the strong desire of so many architects to reestablish a direct and profound relationship with nature and its elements, in contrast to today's materialistic lifestyles and garish architecture, implies the reintroduction of a primitive simplicity, a line that was long represented by Ando. This return to the basics or the prototypical, however, is certainly not a one-way street backward in history; rather, it is a search for a new paradigm in architecture and urbanism with which to better address the paradoxical conditions and experiences of our own time. Ito calls his own residence a cluster of primitive huts and considers this as the most suitable architectural model for contemporary urban citizens, who tend to be "nomads" (23).[56]

As Koji Taki has observed, Ito possesses a "mindset

23. Toyo Ito, Egg of Winds, Europalia Exhibition, Brussels, 1989

capable of producing departure [from, as well as], deformations and discrepancies [of], the city-as-is. His chosen method is one of 'slipping.' From early on, Ito composed interiors not by division of rooms, but as fluid passages, to discover living, non-rigid spaces. One extreme extension of this approach is the idea that the fixed domicile has lost its meaning in the contemporary city; a thinking that developed not in disregard of our lifestyles but as a direct result of inquiries into how we live.... Recognizing that no one is really without fixed residence, Ito nonetheless pretextualizes an image of the urban nomad, albeit not so much to posit a literally uprooted city, as to depict an image of liberation from political and authoritarian constraint."[57] Thus, Ito's nomadic architecture is also meant to preempt the insidious process of commodification in and by the megalopolis.

Beyond Ito's primitive, yet industrially-fabricated tent structures, many other works remind us of such simple, unpretentious shelters as *yurtas*, huts, and cave or cliff dwellings. In this respect Yamamoto, Hasegawa, Sakamoto, and Kazuyo Sejima's buildings come to mind first, though Yasumitsu Matsunaga's earth architecture with the cylindrical barn-like structures in his Inscription (1987), as well as the numerous tent-like domes over his Daita Housing Project (1989), could also exemplify this direction. However, the evocation of these archaic architectural prototypes is now made possible with the help of light and insubstantial constructs rather than dominant forms. In fact, there is here a manifest disinterest in manipulating forms into anything like designed and unified objects, and in certain cases the architects' concern is very much anti- or non-formal.

The work of Kazuyo Sejima, one of the youngest architects, is an excellent case in point. In her Platform House projects, such as the first completed one, in Katsuura (1988), Sejima works from a position very similar to that of Ito, her former employer and teacher, which aims at removing architecture from the tyranny of composed form and retrospective symbols. This much is clear not only from the apparent lightness and almost ethereal spatial quality of the house, but also from her own words:

"Currently, my attempt is to make architecture overlap with actions that are performed discontinuously. When such momentary actions coincide with locales, a certain volume and a detectable outline are derived. Another moment would bring a new outline. Thus, a definitive, fixed image cannot precede, or emerge out of, the whole process."[58]

While Sejima's designs allude to an architecture as action or event, each of Kazunari Sakamoto's new works is intended to be building-as-environment rather than building-as-object. He explains that "building-as-object depicts a building which has a dominant form...[and whose] meaning...exists in a formal, visual composition. On the other hand, building-as-environment refers to a building which we or something can relate to on some different levels" *(24).*[59] This de-formalization and often de-formation, however, is brought about in several ways. While architects like Ando, Fujii, Suzuki, and Aida employ layered concrete walls and orthogonal frameworks to suspend form or filter the ambient landscape in a discontinuity, others turn to industrially mass-produced, lightweight materials to create thin, membranous boundaries and collage-like, ambiguous enclosures, often with an intended superficiality.[60]

In both cases these designers are able to achieve, though in different ways, a certain perceptual immateriality, or the insubstantiality found in traditional architecture, without resorting to nostalgic or sentimental references to a formal past. Kenneth Frampton in his "Ukiyo-e and the Art of Toyo Ito" observed that Ito's architecture, and by extension the majority of the new avant-garde works, now have that implicit quality that has always characterized Japanese art—especially calligraphy and *ukiyo-e* (pictures of the floating world)—wherein there is no clear distinction between writing and painting; their surfaceness and calligraphic delicacy, just like those of the intricate, thin and semi-transparent layers of the new urban fabric woven by these architects, allude to an invisible depth and unexplainable void, reminiscent of the goal of Buddhist philosophy, which frustrates rationality and causes knowledge or the subject to

24. *Kazunari Sakamoto, Housing Project, Osaka (model, and elevation)*

vacillate.[61]

In other words, while unhesitatingly employing the materials and (high-tech) products of a technologically advanced industry, these architects manage to express opposition to contemporary industrial and consumer society. As a result, we can witness the evolution of a new urban industrial vernacular which promises to provide a meaningful alternative to the fast-escalating megalopolitan project. The works of some other architects, such as Shinohara, Komiyama, Yatsuka, and Maki provide additional information; in their interpretation and response to the new urban landscape, they question deterministic structures by breaking "the imperialism of [their] unity."[62] Yet they do so not to destroy every structure, but rather to attend to a more sensitive and flexible order.

Zero Degree Urban Machine versus the Decentered City

Shinohara, who has changed direction several times during his career, now shows an increased interest in the peculiar qualities of the contemporary city. His early references to the primitive have been replaced, in the 1980s, by the new visions of awkward high-tech machines with a "zero-degree meaning."[63] This does not mean, however, that his new designs completely lack meanings since, as he explains, "these meaningless machines can take on new meanings in architecture"; the fragmentary quality of their forms and structure are charged with a capacity to yield unexpected images which can make sense even under today's fast-changing circumstances.[64] It is this point of understanding where Shinohara's machine is analogous to the surfaceness, random-noise, fragmenta-

tion, and progressive anarchy of the city. Although his buildings still reject the urban chaos, they also draw from the vitality and energy of its resources. The city-as-machine also outlines the vision of a new, information-fueled technopolis (25).

Accordingly, Shinohara's architecture, similar to that of Matsunaga, Takeyama, Komiyama, Yatsuka, Maki and others, is a peculiar expansion of modernism that does away with the false dichotomy between modern and post-modern architecture, and so transcends both. In Maki's case this transcendence is derived from his further investigations into the relationship between the part and the whole. Writing about this with regard to his current architecture, he characterizes the intended environment as an aggregate of active, heterogeneous parts which, while never conforming to a formula, generate the whole.[65] Several of his recent projects, including the Fujisawa Gymnasium (1984), the Spiral Building (1985), and the Makuhari Messe (1989), attest to this intention (26). On the other hand, Maki's National Museum of Modern Art in Kyoto (1986) moves in a somewhat different direction, bringing him closer in line with two other "ex-metabolists": Kurokawa and Isozaki. Within a closed modernist framework and envelope, whose outside grid pattern alludes to Kyoto's ancient urban plan, he has brought together, in a ceremonial though refined manner, explicit references to other episodes of 20th century architecture, such as that of De Stijl and Carlo Scarpa. This manner of explicitly quoting from historic architecture characterizes today not only Isozaki's work but in fact also Kurokawa's, and could be considered as forwarding the cause of post-modernism, rather than as an expansion of modernism.

Beginning with the 1980s, Isozaki's architecture started to show features that had seldom appeared in his works before. This change in direction is exemplified first by the Tsukuba Center Building of 1983. In the 1970s, Isozaki's designs had been unique blends of abstract metaphors and subtle quotations executed in a radical man-

25. *Kazuo Shinohara, Police Headquarters, Kumamoto (model)*

26. *Fumihiko Maki, Fujisawa Gym, Fujisawa, 1984*

ner that consistently opposed mainstream aesthetic trends in architecture, assuring him the leading position in the Japanese avant-garde. Many of his recent works, however, are compositions of a growing number of explicit though cliché-like similes and representational elements from historical Western styles. In other words, he has come much closer to the American, especially Gravesian, populist post-modernist recollections of European classicism, and so, closer to a more conformist architectural as well as political establishment.

This is so even if, as in the large-scale government project of Tsukuba, with its sunken, void, or negative urban plaza, he was to question the authority of the state by eliminating a central symbol, and preempting the notion of center itself. The Tsukuba is unquestionably a significant urban project, yet it already manifests signs of a certain loss, which refer not just to the loss of center, but also to the loss of a previously maintained, more critical attitude of his toward the growing reactionary tendencies of contemporary culture. Kenneth Frampton summed it up this way: "In place of his ironic but nonetheless intellectually challenging and sensuous 'twilight' manner and tectonic rigor of his 'anagrammatic'... forms, Isozaki finds himself reduced, at Tsukuba, to historicist disjunction and syntactical suturing" *(27)*.[66]

A somewhat similar ideological uncertainty characterizes much of Kurokawa's recent architecture as well, which also alludes to the absence of center. Breaking away from his previous and long-maintained role as a radical metabolist, his new designs are less predicated, if predicated at all, on technological phantasmagoria. While this is a welcome development indeed, his explorations of a less structuralist architectural language or the concept of *le poétique* that go beyond semiotics, have not always yielded successful results, breaking no new ground in the field.[67] His philosophy of symbiosis is undeniably correct to point out similarities between particular strains in Buddhist traditions and contemporary French post-structuralist philosophy, and so it is also correct in forwarding a manifest criticism of the domination of Western metaphysics. Yet several of the actual projects, such as the National Bunraku Theater (1983), the Roppongi Prince Hotel (1984), and the Japan-German Centrum in Berlin (1988), are less convincing regarding his implementation of this theory.[68] They prove that merely assembling architectural elements with various historical and cultural references or simulacra, not to mention outright replicas, does not necessarily guarantee new discoveries and the much necessary and essential critical edge of any design.

Nevertheless, Kurokawa also continues his tradition of producing an increasing number of well-polished, high quality public buildings, such as most of his recent museum projects including the ones in Nagoya (1987) and Hiroshima (1988), even if his dramatic conversion from *l'enfant terrible* to establishment architect still seems to impose certain limitations on his work *(28)*. Writing about this architecture, Charles Jencks described the Hi-

27. *Arata Isozaki, Tsukuba Center Building, Tsukuba, 1983*

roshima City Museum as his "most mature and restrained work to date. In the 'sixties and 'seventies his architecture, while inventive and challenging, was often somewhat diagrammatic—an illustration of 'Metabolism,' or 'capsule architecture,' or more recently 'Rikyu gray,' and 'symbiosis.' The Hiroshima Museum, while still an illustration of these concepts, is far more convincing than any theorem: it's a building that persuades one slowly, by stealth, without making any grand statements or propositions."[69]

The Urban Theater

Despite all their evident allusions to modernism and a modernist vocabulary, Maki's museum in Kyoto, and even his Spiral Building in Tokyo, reveal a certain theatricality. This quality, however, is not limited to Maki's architecture; with varying intensity it surfaces in many other works of the new avant-garde. A theatrical lightness is clearly detectable in Yatsuka's Angelo Tarlazzi Building (1987) as well. The elegant dance of architectural fragments in front of the "black canvas" is a gesture that transcends much previous modernist dogma; modern architects would never have accepted such gestures. With Yatsuka, modernism is thus accelerated, pushed to the

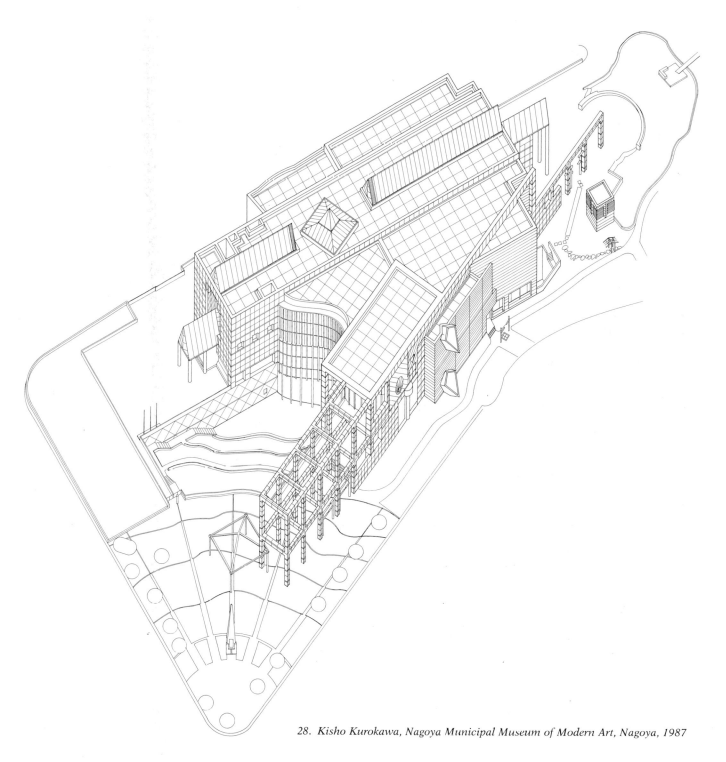

28. Kisho Kurokawa, Nagoya Municipal Museum of Modern Art, Nagoya, 1987

limit and, while rendered largely as a choreographed play of signs, deconstructed.

The theatrical character of Japanese architecture in the late 1980s reaches its epitome in the works of new symbolists such as Osamu Ishiyama, Atsushi Kitagawara and, most especially, Shin Takamatsu. None of them is, however, easily classifiable. Kitagawara, for example,

has a keen sense for fragmentary compositions similar to that of some other Japanese architects such as Yatsuka, Suzuki, and several foreign designers such as Zaha Hadid, Bernard Tschumi, Frank Gehry and Coop Himmelblau (all of them also active in Tokyo). The small mixed-use Building 395 (1986), which includes the architect's studio, attests to such an affinity. On the other

29. *Shin Takamatsu, Week Building, Kyoto, 1986*

hand, Kitagawara's largest complex to date, the Rise (1986) in Tokyo, would appear to demonstrate that he is not always interested in reviving aspects of modernism. Indeed, the Rise expresses nothing of the optimistic positivism with which modernist architects usually approached the problems of urban design. Here, their heroic gestures are supplanted by a nervous and vibrant sensibility that responds to the fragile, theatrical nature of the contemporary city in Japan.

Yet, the collapsing forms of the undulating cast-aluminum drapes on the roof, and all the other fragmented elements of the building, which is, coincidentally, a complex of movie theaters, suggest a temporariness that transcends the simple understanding of the urban environment as merely a continuously changing realm; the Rise foreshadows, if not actually enacts, some forthcoming catastrophe, showing destruction and the inevitability of a ruinous landscape. The aesthetics of catastrophe, or a "feeling of the impossibility for anything to reach a state of completion on its own," is a contemporary experience that informs many works in recent Japanese architecture, from Isozaki to Suzuki, from Hara to Yamamoto, and even from Shinohara to Ito, and which surfaces here once again in a rather explicit, literary manner.[70]

A somewhat similar, albeit seemingly more difficult, intellectual sensibility propels the work of Shin Tak-

amatsu, who is unquestionably the chief protagonist in the escalating and, for him, expressly bizarre urban theater. In the face of the confusion and a growing tendency toward mass cuteness, whereby, as Chris Fawcett observed, "super-naive Western-Romantic effects decorate a good number of urban façades, where stained glass graces the interiors of the Coyer coffee houses, and where wedding halls can be realized with a pretty, girlish flourish," Takamatsu assumes his role basically as an adversary.[71] Accordingly, he makes his buildings into a kind of countershock or sabotage in the city, delivered with bewitching power. Until very recently he achieved this through his fascination with the brutality and unrefined power of the primitive machine. The Ark (1983) and Pharaoh (1984) buildings are evident examples of his metaphors of mechanical darkness or industrial despair. The machine image culminates in the Origin III (1986)—a project Fawcett called "suicide machine"—before exploding and disintegrating in the Week Building (1986). The Week thus enacts the death of the machine and perhaps also that of the First Machine Age *(29).* It is at this "dead tech" where the paths of Takamatsu, Kitagawara, Suzuki, Takasaki, and several other Japanese designers intersect, though on different levels and only momentarily.

While a sinister outlook prevails in the Kirin Plaza (1987), this building also signals another direction in Takamatsu's architecture. It points toward a more sophisticated high-tech urban machine that not only expresses the frightening aspects of an overwhelming technology but speaks equally of the vitality and fictional quality of the ever-changing story of the city. The Kirin is a tower of both darkness and light, and is as cryptic as it is sensuous, as morbid as it is fun, or as much a nightmare as a daydream; in it Takamatsu seems to comment, as in the early stages of his career, not only on matters of death, but also of life, and in this sense, it is a paradoxical but significant architectural and urban statement. Yet, despite all the intended critiques of our urban predicament reflected in the uninhibited antagonisms and mysterious obscurity of his "difficult" designs, Takamatsu faces a dilemma: his buildings are now on their way to being worshipped and turned into temples of consumption by the very culture he wants to escape. This is, however, a dilemma that no architect can completely evade today.

Through the various interpretations of the urban theater, therefore, runs the thread of a peculiar threshold that both divides and binds together the notions of progress and decadence—or rather, of reality and fiction—while eliciting new design sensibilities. Most Japanese architects intuitively understand that the proper staging of the urban realm and the human life within depends on the simultaneous acting of two forces or tendencies: one enables the city continuously to renew itself and maintain its multiple presences, the other makes it possible for the city to clear the stage for the next act by pulling down the set and debris of the previous scenario. In fact, for the Japanese, these two things—that is to say, building and demolition, or construction and deconstruction—are one and the same thing, which is as paradoxical as the notion of progressive decadence, or decadence with vitality.[72] This should remind us again that the Japanese tend to apprehend things as events rather than as substance.[73]

Nevertheless, this is the aspect of Japanese architecture which, as we have seen previously, is the most vulnerable to consumerist exploitation. With this the circle of events seems to be complete (or, the circuits closed?), constituting the predicament of present architecture and urbanism in Japan. Therefore, the new avant-garde faces an immense task in reversing the pervasiveness and inertia of the megalopolitan project, and its success is both problematic and limited at the moment. Yet, there seems to be hope in that a new strategy is evolving among the various approaches and attempts. This strategy is reminiscent of the method Michel Foucault followed in the later part of his philosophical enterprise. In it, Foucault combined "a type of *archaeological* analysis which preserves the distancing [or critical] effect of structuralism, and an interpretive [poetic] dimension which develops the hermeneutic insight that the investigator is always situated and must understand the meaning of his cultural practices [also] from within them.... Thus, Foucault manage[d] both to criticize and to utilize—in a highly original way—the two

dominant methods available for the study of human beings," and, it may be added, for the shaping of the human environment.[74]

In other words, the success of the Japanese avant-garde in creating a more liberating environment in the city will rest on those practices which, by way of their sheer guts, probity, and determination to resist the nightmare of progress, are able to initiate and extend critical interstices in an otherwise instrumental world, predicated on the logic of consumption.

NOTES
1. Fumihiko Maki, "Spiral," *Japan Architect* (March, 1987), p. 33.
2. Under the Tokugawa shogunate, Japan was closed to the outside world from 1639 until 1853 when Commodore Perry forced Japan to reopen her gates and eventually resume relations with the West.
3. When Buddhism was introduced to Japan from China via Korea in the mid–6th century AD, the Japanese adopted many elements of Chinese culture and civilization, including their writing system, arts and architecture, city planning, the model of government and state apparatus. This purposeful borrowing by the Japanese, though with varying intensity, continued for centuries until the Tokugawa era.
4. Among the first foreign architects were the Englishman, Josiah Conder (1852–1920); the Frenchman, C. de Boinville; the Italian, C. V. Capelletti; and the German, Hermann Ende. Visiting Western architects, including Frank Lloyd Wright, Antonin Raymond, Bruno Taut, and Walter Gropius continued to exert a profound influence on Japanese architecture.
5. Noboru Kawazoe, *Contemporary Japanese Architecture* (Tokyo: Kokusai Bunka Shinkokai, 1965), p. 19.
6. Industrialization did gradually alter the landscape and the urbanscape even before the War, but its impact on the overall "order" of the cities was far less than during the economic boom of the 1950s and 1960s, when "the reality of urban planning," as William Coaldrake pointed out, "was gruesomely pragmatic, opportunistic, and self-serving." From "Order and Anarchy: Tokyo from 1868 to the Present," in Martin Friedman, ed., *Tokyo: Form and Spirit* (New York: Abrams, 1986), p. 71.
7. Despite the many large-scale urban planning proposals, Tokyo's general street pattern and the configuration of many of its districts reveal persistent continuities with the past; much of the present "structure" of Tokyo derives from the older castle town of Edo. This can be attributed to the fact that Japan does *not* have deep-rooted and widespread urban planning traditions, and despite all the many initiatives, "most attempts to implement conventional planning strategies failed," even after World War II. From David Stewart, *The Making of a Modern Japanese Architecture: 1868 to the Present* (Tokyo and New York: Kodansha International, 1987), p. 172.
8. Toyo Ito, "In Search of a Context, 1971-," *Japan Architect* (April, 1982), p. 22.
9. At Kurokawa's Nakagin Capsule Building (1972) in Tokyo, for example, one prefabricated and ready-made studio apartment unit cost as much as a Toyota sedan of the day and could be ordered and purchased in a similar way: with a variety of optional packages according to the taste of the consumer.
10. Fumihiko Maki, "The Theory of Group Form," *Japan Architect* (February, 1970), p. 39.

11. Roland Barthes, *Empire of Signs* trans. Richard Howard (New York: Hill and Wang, 1982).

12. Ibid, p. 36.

13. The layout of the Chinese city corresponded to the Hindu and esoteric Buddhist cosmic order and world concept: the sky or heaven was regarded as round and the earth rectangular, its four sides coinciding with the cardinal points of the compass; the realm of in-between was assigned to man.

14. For example, in these Japanese capitals, city walls were erected only partially or not at all, and even when they were, the incomplete segments had a symbolic rather than actual defensive role. Furthermore, the western parts of both Nara and Kyoto did not develop simultaneously with the eastern sections, and in Nara became permanently abandoned. Thus, present day Nara occupies only the northeastern part of the originally planned capital.

15. Previously planned, but short-term capitals were: Naniwa (645–667); Otsu (667–694); Fujiwara (694–710); Heijō (or Nara 710–784); Kuni (740–745); and Nagaoka (784–794).

16. The term *sophisticated order* was coined by Gunter Nitschke in his seminal essay "MA - The Japanese Sense of Place," *AD, Architectural Design* (March, 1966), pp. 147–148.

17. William Coaldrake, "Order and Anarchy: Tokyo from 1868 to the Present," Friedman, *Tokyo: Form and Spirit*, op. cit., p. 72. Many castles were demolished after 1615 by the order of Tokugawa Ieyasu, the military shogun, to prevent internal fighting among feudal landlords that jeopardized the just-achieved political unification of the country. Other castles were razed by World War II. Today there are only some twelve remaining or rebuilt castles.

18. In the history of Japanese architecture and urbanism, we cannot speak about *public* buildings in the conventional sense. Such buildings did not develop until the modern era. Stoas, stadia, town halls, libraries, and other facilities for people to gather have always been missing in Japan. "The theaters, magistrates' offices, and schools that appeared in the Edo period were all auxiliary facilities of samurai residences, temples, or shrines, and were architecturally only variations of the latter group of buildings." From Fumihiko Maki, "The Public Dimension in Contemporary Architecture," *Maki, Isozaki—New Public Architecture: Recent Projects by Fumihiko Maki and Arata Isozaki* (New York: The Japan Society, 1985), p. 16 (catalog of exhibition).

19. Fujimori Terunobu, "Urban Planning in the Meiji Era," in Shuji Takashina, ed., *Tokyo: Creative Chaos*, Special Issue of *Japan Echo* (Vol. XIV, 1987), p. 49.

20. Shuji Takashina, ibid, p. 5.
It also has to be pointed out that the Japanese-built landscape—architecture and gardens, not to mention the urbanscape—has always been characterized by a uniquely *fragmented* quality. As observed, the line of vision and physical movement through space is consistently obscured or broken; the stroll garden thus is but an aggregate of "independent" vistas with "unrelated" events. Even in the tiny tea room (*chashitsu*), a small wall (*sodekabe*) obstructs the view of the whole space, covering one of the corners in a curious way.

21. Vladimir Krstic, "A Life Act and Urban Scenography: Supraphysical Concept of Urban Form in the Core of the Japanese City," master thesis, department of architecture, Kyoto University, 1985, p. 17.

22. In the history of Japanese architecture, not only were capitals moved frequently, but also buildings disassembled and rebuilt at another location. Buildings also had to be rebuilt after natural or other disasters, often several times during their his-

tory. In addition, Shinto shrines were periodically and regularly rebuilt as part of the purification ritual, a custom observed today only in the renowned Ise shrine.

23. Toyo Ito, "Collage and Superficiality in Architecture," in Kenneth Frampton, ed., *A New Wave of Japanese Architecture*, IAUS Catalog No. 10, (New York: IAUS, 1978), p. 68.

24. According to Zen Buddhist teachings, "Form is emptiness and emptiness is form," alluding to ultimate nothingness, or a "plural void" that contains the personal "I" and everything else, and toward which Buddhist conduct leads.

25. Vladimir Krstic, "A Life Act," op. cit., pp. 36–37.

26. Ibid, p. 52.

27. Toyo Ito's words in "Kazuo Shinohara," in *Shinkenchiku* (special issue on the houses of the Showa period), 1976.

28. It is revealing to read the writings, reflections, or commentaries of these architects; almost all would refer to the contemporary conditions of the city in one way or another. Many architects, such as Maki, Shinohara, Ito, Ando, Hasegawa, Yamamoto, Takamatsu, Kitagawara, or Suzuki derive much of their architectural thoughts and design philosophies from critically addressing the issue of urbanism in Japan.

29. Kenneth Frampton, "Towards a Critical Regionalism," in Hal Foster, ed., *The Anti-Aesthetic* (Port Townsend: Bay Press, 1983), p. 20.

30. Hajime Yatsuka, "Architecture in the Urban Desert," *Oppositions*, No. 23 (Winter, 1981), p. 20.

31. Chris Fawcett calls the Japanese megalopolis "Japan-the-city" in his *New Japanese House* (New York: Harper and Row, 1980), p. 31.

32. The "New Wave of Japanese Architecture" was an exhibition that toured several cities in the United States and Europe from late 1978 to early 1979. It introduced the variety of new movements that replaced metabolist architecture in Japan around the early '70s.

33. Botond Bognar, *Contemporary Japanese Architecture: Its Development and Challenge* (New York: Van Nostrand Reinhold, 1985), p. 277.

34. Tadao Ando, "Town House at Kujo," *Japan Architect* (Nov.-Dec., 1983), p. 52.

35. It has to be pointed out that the respective architecture of these designers was extensively shaped by numerous other, rather divergent, intentions and design philosophies as well.

36. Hiroshi Hara, "On the Form of Reflection Houses," *G. A. Document*, (Special Issue, 1970–80).

37. Hiroshi Hara, "Anti-Traditional Architectural Contrivance," Frampton, *A New Wave of Japanese Architecture*, op. cit., p. 39.

38. Itsuko Hasegawa, "Embedding Architecture in the City," *Shinkenchiku*, June 1978.

39. The term "le poétique" has been extensively used by contemporary French post-structuralist philosophers, especially Julia Kristeva, Gilles Deleuze, and Jean Baudrillard. See, for example, J. Kristeva, *La Revolution du Langage Poétique* (Paris: Le Seuil, 1974).

40. Marc Treib, "The Dichotomies of Dwelling: Edo/Tokyo," Friedman, *Tokyo: Form and Spirit*, op. cit., p. 121.

41. Kenneth Frampton, "The Work of Tadao Ando," in Yukio Futagawa, ed., *Tadao Ando* (Tokyo: A.D.A. EDITA, 1987), p. 10.

42. Tadao Ando, "From Self-Enclosed Modern Architecture Towards Universality," *Japan Architect* (May, 1982), p. 9.

43. Hiromi Fujii, "Architectural Metamorphology," *Oppositions* No. 22 (1980); "Deconstruction through Differentiation—Metamorphology, Desemiotization, Traces and Deconstruction," *Japan Architect*, (September, 1985); "De-composition," *A + U, Ar-*

chitecture and Urbanism, (January, 1980).

44. Hiromi Fujii, "Dispersed, Multilayered Space," Japan Architect (January, 1989), p. 6.

45. Hiroshi Hara, "Modality—Central Concept of Contemporary Architecture," Japan Architect (November/December, 1986), p. 24.

46. Ibid, p. 26.

47. Takefumi Aida, "From Toy-Blocks to an Architecture of Fluctuation," Shinkenchiku (June, 1987), p. 203.

48. Itsuko Hasegawa, "Thin Membranous Boundaries," Japan Architect (November/December, 1986), p. 54.

49. Yasumitsu Matsunaga, "T House." See in this volume.

50. Ibid.

51. Koji Taki, "Fragments and Noise: The Architectural Ideas of Kazuo Shinohara and Toyo Ito," Architectural Design: Japanese Architecture (Vol. 58, No. 5/6, 1988), p. 34.

52. Fumihiko Maki, "To Offer Unforgettable Scenes," (A Discussion with Fumihiko Maki), Japan Architect (March, 1987), p. 69.

53. Riken Yamamoto, "The City as Topography," Japan Architect, (November/December, 1986), p. 42.

54. Contemporary Architecture in Drawings, 11—Space and Concept: Ryoji Suzuki (Tokyo: Dohosha, 1986), p. 3.

55. Hiroshi Watanabe, "High-Tech Shangri-la," GA Document, No. 17 (1987).

56. Toyo Ito, "Primitive Hut in the Modern City," Japan Architect (May, 1985), p. 30.

57. Koji Taki, "Fragments and Noise," Architectural Design-Japanese Architecture, op. cit., 51, p. 34.

58. Kazuyo Sejima, "Platform No. 1, Katsuura, 1988." See in this volume. The manuscript originally entitled "Architectural Place."

59. Kazunari Sakamoto, "From Architecture as an Object to Space as an Environment," Japan Architect (November/December, 1986), p. 64.

60. See, for example, Toyo Ito, "Collage and Superficiality in Architecture," Frampton, A New Wave of Japanese Architecture, op. cit., p. 68.

61. Kenneth Frampton, "Ukiyo-e and the Art of Toyo Ito," Space Design, (September, 1986), p. 144.
Frampton employed the term ukiyo-e in relation to Ito's architecture for two reasons; "firstly, because the Japanese wood block print (Ukiyo-e) was a middle class art created for a middle class throughout the Tokugawa period (1603–1868) and in that sense it was quintessentially an art for the people and by people; secondly, because such prints project a floating, transient world redolent in many respects of the same spiritual stoicism and energy which Ito displays toward the Megalopolis."

62. The term "imperialism of unity" is used in Paul Ricoeur, History and Truth (Evanston: Northwestern University Press, 1965), p. xxi.

63. Kazuo Shinohara, "A Program for the 'Fourth Space,'" Japan Architect, (September, 1986), p. 28.

64. Ibid.

65. Fumihiko Maki, "Modernism at the Crossroad," Japan Architect (March, 1983), p. 22.

66. Kenneth Frampton, "Twilight Gloom to Self-Enclosed Modernity: Five Japanese Architects," Friedman, Tokyo: Form and Spirit, op. cit., p. 225.

67. Kisho Kurokawa, "Le Poétique in Architecture: Beyond Semiotics," Process Architecture, Kisho Kurokawa: Recent Works and Projects, No. 66 (1986) p. 154.

68. Kurokawa, "The Philosophy of Symbiosis: From Internationalism to Interculturalism," ibid, p. 48.

69. Charles Jencks, "Hiroshima Acropolis," Space Design (June, 1989), Special Issue, Kisho Kurokawa: 1979–1989, p. 6.

70. Riichi Miyake, "The Generation of Sensitiveness," Japan Architect, (November/December, 1986), p. 10.
Ryoji Suzuki, "An 'Archipolitique' of Architecture," Japan Architect, (October, 1987), p. 36.

71. Chris Fawcett, "Architecture: The Essential Scandal: Three recent works by Shin Takamatsu," (manuscript, 1984), p. 1.

72. In this respect it is instructive to read one of Isozaki's early short writings "The City Demolition Industry, Inc.," from 1962. In it, Isozaki as architect and urban designer continues a most interesting dialogue with his personal alter ego, Shin (the other reading of the Chinese character of Arata, his first name), a subversive element who specializes in fragmenting, demolishing, or destroying cities. As the debate ends with a "no win" situation between the "adversaries," Isozaki was able to convey rather poignantly his ambivalent relationship toward the Japanese megalopolis. (This article is reprinted in Frampton, A New Wave of Japanese Architecture, op. cit., p. 48.) This paradoxical attitude of Isozaki is also expressed in one of his "City in the Sky" projects of the same year, in which ruins of ancient classical architecture (the poetry of ruin) are superimposed on the visions of the city of the future (Fig. 4).

73. Seen from a Western perspective, much of Japanese culture could indeed appear outright "decadent." No other culture has ever been more predisposed toward the aesthetics and artistic appreciation of such notions as transitoriness, aging, withering away, and even decay, than the Japanese has all through its history. Such predisposition is complemented by the Japanese impulse and readiness toward relocating, rebuilding structures, and also capitals, with or without numerous devastating natural or man-inflicted disasters, and by their attitude toward "absence" and self-effacement (also in the form of suicide). Yet all these have not necessarily been interpreted as unequivocally negative aspects of life. The process of destruction and decadence, in this sense, has been regarded both as a continuous phenomenon and as a precondition for the perpetual change, renewal and, paradoxically enough, of the continuity of things.
Francesco Dal Co, talking about the issues of "fullness vs. decadence" in a recent interview ("On History and Architecture"), has outlined a very similar interpretation by saying: "Typically, the by-product of [the] characteristically Western idea [of incline and decline] is an understanding and description of history as a sequence of events figured by moments of fullness and moments of absence or decadence....[Yet] we have to accept that all moments in history are connected, that there are no real boundaries between moments of fullness and decadence; that fullness and decadence are not only connected to each other, they are implied or contained within each other." From Perspecta, no. 23, p. 14.

74. Hubert L. Dreyfus and Paul Rabinow, Michel Foucault: Beyond Structuralism and Hermeneutics (Chicago: University of Chicago Press, 1983), pp. xiii and xxvii. (emphasis mine).

AN ARCHITECTURE FLOATING ON THE SEA OF SIGNS

Hajime Yatsuka

For contemporary architects, Japanese cities have presented different faces throughout the decades. In the 1960s, the period of Japan's first rapid economic growth, cities appeared as physical structures to be interfered with or, conversely, to be built as huge "buildings." Such interpretation characterized the architecture of Kenzo Tange and the metabolist group, for example.[1] In the 1970s, when, after the economic crisis, the pace of building activity slowed down considerably, the urban realm emerged as a merely alienating, anonymous, and hostile environment, to which architects were prompted to react negatively, while trying to maintain an identity of their own, in most cases by way of small but provocative works. Thereafter, in the 1980s, in the present period of Japan's second economic resurrection—a resurrection that this time is taking place practically only in that country—the city has become something which lies beyond its physical aspects; it is now regarded as a locus for signification, a phenomenon I would like to call the "sea of signs."

Tokyo today is assuming a role that was played by Paris as "the capital of the 19th century" in the 1880s, and by New York as the "New Babylon" in the 1960s; it is now the capital of a new *fin de siècle*, but, unlike Paris and New York, in a post-modern way.[2] In terms of physical structure, Tokyo lacks things grandiose, such as the grand boulevards of Paris or the majestic skyscrapers of New York, which were indispensable settings for the great capitals of the modern era. Instead, Tokyo is a vast accumulation of mediocre structures; it is a city without character, something like Franz Kafka's castle. Nevertheless, this accumulation is not necessarily a systematic layering of the strata of preceding periods. Tradition, if any remains, has been violated and by now almost abandoned. The most symptomatic examples of this development are the numerous occasions when Tokyo burned to ashes, as it did in World War II. Yet, unlike all European cities after the war, Tokyo was rebuilt almost without any adherence to its ancient structures or historic buildings. Moreover, the reconstruction work and the following building policies have, more than ever before, compounded the quality of Japanese cities as patchworks of eclectic mixtures.

Patchwork here means that there is no organic relationship between neighboring elements such as streets and buildings, and that it is not possible to establish such a relationship. According to the viewpoint of modern town planning and its blind obsession with restoring the "sick" city into a healthy and rationally ordered one, these accidental characteristics of "patchwork" were simply unacceptable and had to be rejected. Nevertheless, such a rational attitude was not the invention of modernism; a similar understanding also shaped the concept of the traditional European city throughout the history of Western architecture. On the contrary, today's post-modernism (which in the sense used here has nothing to do with the trifling with the vocabulary of European classicism), in discarding the aspiration to completeness, has made the patchwork a new object of interest.

The French philosopher Gilles Deleuze has borrowed the term *corps sans organes* (a body without organs) from Antonin Artaud to refer to the organizational or, to be more precise, anti-organizational system of patchwork.[3] This term then has also been coupled with another one, which is Deleuze's own "rhizome."[4] "Rhizome" rejects every kind of hierarchical order; it is a more radical model of the relationship among components than "semi-lattice," which was formulated by Christopher Alexander as an antithesis to the hierarchical "tree." For Alexander, "a city is not a tree," but a set of semi-lattices, a more complex organization.[5] However, a semi-lattice is still an agglomeration of tree-like subsets, and therefore it is not really an antithesis of the "tree." On the other hand, a "rhizome" rebels against all kinds of hierarchy. It lacks any sense of organization. Thus, in the *corps sans organes*, or "rhizome," each component lacks the synthesized connection to others; it is a patchwork.

Deleuze himself compares the notion of patchwork to that of texture, a term that has been often used as a metaphor of the city. Thus he seems to suggest that the tendency is to move from the texture to the patchwork, from the synthesized city to the city *sans organes*, from *la ville radieuse* to the patchwork city of anarchy.[6] Such is the direction of change in the urban conditions of Japan that prepares the ground work, or context, for contemporary Japanese architecture. One could actually call these developments the conditions of the post-modern city. And as most other aspects of post-modernism in Japan, the post-modernity of contemporary Japanese cities is inseparably entangled with the country's premodern urban conditions.

Tokyo, called Edo before the 1868 Meiji restoration, was historically the administrative capital of the Tokugawa Shogunate. The general layout of Japanese feudal towns followed two types of organization: the first was based on a gridiron pattern inherited from the ancient capitals such as Kyoto and Nara, while the second was the outcome of a maze-like street pattern, the genuine invention of the feudal period. The maze pattern, though

conceived along purely functional, i.e., defensive considerations to prevent enemy invasion, can be regarded as a curious predecessor of today's "rhizome." In the Meiji period (1868–1912), restructuring Tokyo, the previous city of the Shogun, by devising projects for grand boulevards and an efficient traffic system to match prominent Western cities like Paris and Berlin, was almost an obsession with the Japanese government. However, such ambitions never really bore fruit at the time, nor on such later occasions as after the war or the big earthquake of 1923.

On the contrary, the dramatic increase of land value has fostered the subdivision of land, and along with it, further contributed to the fragmentation and irregularity of the urban fabric; landowners, trying to avoid heavy tax increases, have been forced to sell portions of their property or build something on it in order to make a profit. The building cost of the unit floor area, no matter how luxurious the building, is now no more than the annual tax of the land of the same unit area. Of course, this phenomenon is characteristic of the 1980s, and more particularly of their latter half, and so, one still finds old town houses or even ancient shrines tucked here and there among the recent commercial or office buildings. Uniformity within the districts is the last thing to expect. Size, forms, colors, and use differ from building to building. Each building is a patchwork in the district which is itself a patchwork in the city. This kind of unevenness lays bare a cross-section of Japan's economic strata.

Traditionally, the imagery of the future city within the dream of utopia was conceived as a complete entity of homogeneous components, with every building and every district depicted as if planned by a particular person and built at once. Modern utopias, including the cities conceived by the master builders of the 1920s, were no exception. But the radical heterogeneity of contemporary Japanese cities is exactly the opposite, and testify to the failure of the "enlightened project" of modernism as advocated by Jürgen Habermas.[7] Such uneven heterogeneity seems to represent the absurdity of the automatic course of capitalist development which rejects all kinds of rational intervention, and which maintains the messy disorder of the pre- or early-capitalist structures of the city—an accusation also forwarded by such modernists as Le Corbusier.

However, should the absence of the powerful planning discipline always be attributed to only the anachronism or "ruthlessness" of capitalist speculation? The answer, most certainly in Japan, seems to be no, referring to a condition that forms the basis of Japanese architecture in the 1980s. If any new finding has surfaced in the 1980s, it appears to be none other than the fact that Japanese people, too, and not just architects, have begun to notice and find this *ville sans organes* potentially interesting for the first time since the Meiji Restoration. In this decade, one of Japanese post-modernism's most characteristic phenomena is the amazing amount of books about the city by authors from various fields and disciplines; each seems to compete with the others in finding new ways of "reading" the city.[8]

Undoubtedly, the interest in the preservation of historical buildings, which has actually come somewhat too late, has played a certain role in this heightened attention to urban architecture and culture in Japan. Nevertheless, this attention has not yielded any systematic attitude or approach comparable to the rigorous and rational academic research of European architects and historians that is based on the typology of buildings and the morphology of cities. In the chaotic Japanese urban environment, with the exception perhaps of such ancient capitals as Kyoto or Nara, both of which evaded fatal destruction by the War, such concepts have proved to be impotent; *ville sans organes* refutes the possibility of applying the methods of both topology and morphology, which are basically related to the *organes*. Some architects and historians began to devote much attention to second rate buildings, and have found them quite interesting. For them, these mediocre structures play important roles in the city and are not necessarily inferior to the more prominent historic monuments. In fact, the urban conditions of Tokyo are overwhelmingly constituted by "mediocre buildings in a mediocre city," yet it is a most stimulating city.

It is not the first time in the history of modern architecture that a "mediocre" city has become the focus of architects' attention. We have as precedent, for example, Robert Venturi's ironical praise for "ugly and ordinary" architecture.[9] However, Venturi's city, with its commercial strip, was a rather homogeneous and simple agglomeration of recently developed buildings. Compared to it, Japanese cities are comprised of far too many and far more heterogeneous components; they radically lack norms, or even ethics, of their own. This absence of norms can successfully nullify the act of Venturian irony. In these cities, everything could be accepted or, on the contrary, nothing could be effective and justifiable. "Rhizome" is the very idea of freedom from value. In the *ville sans organes*, or in the "city without character," therefore, it is quite difficult, if not impossible, to talk of value.

Another important aspect of contemporary Japanese cities, especially such monstrous ones as Tokyo and Osaka, is that most of their recent developments are also propelled by a rapid process of consumerism typical of the dynamic, though sometimes disorderly, megalopolitan urban centers in advanced, late-capitalist societies. In this respect too, Japanese cities are fragmented, trivialized, and accelerated versions of Venturi's Las Vegas.[10] In the "city of consumption," architecture tends to become a flow of images rather than a stock of buildings. Inasmuch as this consumerist process is related, both explicitly and implicitly, to the circuit of human desire, architecture necessarily symbolizes this desire in a profound way; it acquires the quality of signs rather than substance. Cities are now very complicated circuits of information and desire, which I call the "sea of signs," and through this invisible and multi-layered network of

information flow they act as *loci* for consumption. If Japanese cities could be called "rhizomes," it would be because this system of information and desire is laid over and imbues the totality of architecture. Buildings today, more than ever, are an integral part of this invisible circuit. Although, no doubt, they still exist as real entities, they have already lost integrity, and lack the dimension of "depth" which, of course, is the common feature of the media. "Architecture as media," an axiom advocated as an assumptive theory some thirty years ago, now seems to be turned into reality without any reservation.

All this has created a very ambiguous and problematic situation for architects. On the other hand, it is undeniable that this city of consumption and media has provided them with good opportunities for commissions. In recent commercial mass media, not only their works, but also their own personalities have become frequent subjects of coverage and exposure. This is something rather new for Japanese architects who, unlike novelists and artists, have never been concerned with publicity. An increased public interest in architecture, through the help of the mass media, is one of the most important features of Japan's post-modern condition. Such heightened interest has also prepared the way for the introduction and activity in Japan of a growing number of celebrated foreign architects, such as Michael Graves, Norman Foster, Richard Rogers, Renzo Piano, Hans Hollein, Zaha Hadid, and Rem Koolhaas. This public attention itself is of course welcome. Yet, it goes without saying that such phenomena of popular interest in highly developed consumer societies are inevitably accompanied by the strong tendency of the most conspicuous things, in our case architecture, to become the best commodities. In such a situation today, architects not only produce consumer goods but become, themselves, subjects of the process of consumption, inasmuch as they too have to obey, even if not consciously, the rule of the capitalist society. This is to say, they have to accelerate the most basic condition of consumption, which is an eternal desire for something new. And, along such "imperatives," architecture, to put it simply, becomes a form of fashion and commodity.

This simple fact then also touches upon the other side of the dilemma that architects face today. It is true that the exceptionally loose structure and character of Japanese cities can provide a rather generous medium for those architects who are compelled to come up with something novel. However, in the "city without character," in which it is almost impossible to talk about value, any kind of creative, and even critical manifestation is destined to be absorbed in the void of relativism so thoughtlessly advocated by the protagonists of post-modernism. Beautiful buildings could still be interesting, but only in the same way as mediocre ones can. This is a profoundly paradoxical, if not ironical situation. Once detached from the collective ideal, what Jean-François Lyotard termed the "master narrative," or "grand story" of high-modernism, even the most creative works can only be exceptional in their own "hermetic" way.[11] In other words, these exceptional works "floating on the sea of signs" are only relatively exceptional and are without ultimate character or destination. Therefore, today's seemingly gay orgy of creativity and architectural demonstration necessarily borders on the darkness of nihilism. Yet, it is only in such a borderline situation, a metaphorical tightrope over the abyss, that architects can hope to go on creating or performing the delicate "dance" of their own.

NOTES

1. Metabolist architects, such as Kenzo Tange, Kiyonori Kikutake, and Kisho Kurokawa, the last representatives of Japanese high-modernism, devised large-scale and utopian schemes with megastructures and megaforms, in their attempts to radically restructure existing urban formations.

2. Walter Benjamin, *Charles Baudelaire: Ein Lyriker im Zeitalter des Hochkapitalismus*, Rolf Tiedemann (ed.) (Frankfurt/Main: Suhrkamp, 1974) and Manfredo Tafuri, "New Babylon" (German translation), *Archithese*, no. 20.

3. Gilles Deleuze & Félix Guattari, *Mille Plateaux* (Paris: Les Editions de Minuit, 1980). (Especially in the chapter "Le Lisse et strie.") Also published in English as *A Thousand Plateaus-Capitalism and Schizophrenia*, translation and Foreword by Brian Massumi (Minneapolis: University of Minnesota Press, 1987).

4. Ibid.

5. Christopher Alexander, et. al., *A Pattern Language: Towns, Buildings, Construction* (New York: Oxford University Press, 1977).

6. Gilles Deleuze, *Mille Plateaux*.

7. Jurgen Habermas, "Modernity—An Incomplete Project," in Hal Foster, ed., *The Anti-Aesthetic: Essays on Postmodern Culture* (Port Townsend: Bay Press, 1983), p. 3.

8. I am referring to several books and articles by such authors as Terunobu Fujimori and others. See for example the Special Issue of *Japan Echo*, Vol. XIV (1987) entitled *Tokyo: Creative Chaos*, which contains essays by Fujimori, Takashina Shuji, Hidenobu Jinnai, Akira Naito, Nobuo Fujii, etc.

9. Robert Venturi, Denise Scott Brown, Steven Izenour, *Learning from Las Vegas* (Cambridge: MIT Press, 1972), p. 91.

10. Ibid.

11. Jean-François Lyotard, *The Postmodern Condition: A Report on Knowledge* (Minneapolis: University of Minnesota Press, 1984, ed.), p. xxiii.

FROM THE SAVAGE TO THE NOMAD: CRITICAL INTERVENTIONS IN CONTEMPORARY JAPANESE ARCHITECTURE

Lynne Breslin

IN THE early 20th century the artistic avant-garde appropriated primitivism to mediate its present. The Russian futurists used the peasants' *lubok* (primitive wood block print) and the early icons. For the cubists and European avant-garde painters, the so-called primitive art of Africa, Oceania, and the Americas was rendered with full depiction of the psycho-sexual forces that Freud and anthropology, the latter yet in its infancy, discussed. Dada focused on another primitive—the child and his babble. Piaget worked almost in tandem, discovering development in behavior. In the 1930 book, *L'art primitif*, G. H. Luguet asserted that "the art of children and the art of the primitive man form a single category, one which contests the values of 'civilized art.'"[1]

The analysis of the relationship of these "others" and the art they inspire has continued in the post-structuralist era. The early 20th century's appropriation of the primitive has been recast. Now the focus of post-structuralism, these other cultures—the savage, the nomad, the woman and the child—are examined not as formal paradigms (rhythm) or as original sexual, psy-chological models exposed through historicist or scientific probing, but as alternative epistemes, no longer hierarchically regulated to a line of succession. Each wave of avant-gardism seems to reevaluate the primitive in relation to its own objectives.

The newest wave of "primitivism" in Japanese architecture stems directly from a reading and integration of current structuralist and post-structuralist theory. This has not always been so. Japanese architects have begun again, before. Successive waves of renegotiation of basic elements in design have been undertaken in quest of spiritual renewal. Somehow that primitivism, rather than searching for a distant or "displaced" *time*, usually situated a distant *place*—a landscape of untouched primal nature and beauty. The obsession with the totem (an anthropomorphic object), central to Western primitivism, is absent in Japanese art. Sen-no-Rikyu's retreat from the ornate, overly complicated world of the shogun in the late 16th century may have been stimulated by a wish to escape to a simpler and earlier society, but he visualized a simplified landscape. This focus on a rarefied nature provided a powerful paradigm for later generations of disaffected architects. The concepts of *sabi* and *wabi* circumscribed his tea ceremony, and isolated the most basic elements and landscape. Wood, fire, herbs, and earth were endowed with singular symbolic import and a harmony between nature and art was exacted through restraint, sobriety, simplicity, and a poverty that "surpassed riches." The austerity and spiritual discipline of Zen reached its culmination in tiny wooden huts with thatched roofs and in minutely prescribed rituals of tea. The rustic sensibility of the *sukiya* tea house became established as an architectural ideal *(30)*.

In Western architecture, past surges of primitivism heralded a significant reconsideration of its origins. *Originism* became, from Wren on, a normative tool in architecture. Laugier's "primitive hut"—a rebuff to rococo excesses—proposed a reevaluation of beauty in architecture and the importance of structure for theory. Subsequent rustic episodes occurring at points of critical juncture have signaled a change in architectural epistemes. In contrast, the essential components of Japanese primitivism and its accompanying emphasis on the natural were institutionalized. Beauty in Japanese architecture and art was bound to the *elemental*. The future "cleaning of house" became, aesthetically, a means of returning to what remained at the heart of Japanese beauty in architecture.

Post-war Japanese modern architecture reverberates with a simultaneous recalling of the elemental as a means of maintaining autonomy in the face of universalizing anonymity.[2] The use of French structuralist and post-structuralist criticism has transformed some traditional elements of Japanese "primitivism." The differences between Western and Eastern primitivism have been diffused. Western modernism is seen as very much a legacy for the postwar generations of Japanese architects.

Kazuo Shinohara is representative of this phenom-

30. Tea room, Shokintei, Katsura Villa, Kyoto, 1620–1647

enon in his struggle with the legacy of the Japanese architectural tradition. He emerges from the battle only gradually but his spoils direct the course of his future architectural investigation. His initial discovery of the operation of traditional aesthetics and space, together with the spiritual content it produces, mobilizes the "primitive" in his work and is analyzed in his reflections on the Zen temple:

A stone garden attached to the temple surprises the viewer by its sheer reduction, leaving only a few rocks meticulously distributed across the surface of the white sand. There is a type of chashitsu *with a space for only two mats where all potential action is, so to speak, formally frozen into inaction. I often feel awe before the tenacity of spirit with which the Japanese have so relentlessly pursued formal economy and the process of simplification, never relaxing their hold until they succeed in realizing the ultimate scintillating space. What a strange sort of devotion, and in what an unusual direction. The Japanese have never shown much interest in assembling or transforming given material elements for the purpose of integration and enrichment. Instead, they have often chosen to rob these elements of their vitality, thereby reducing them to inorganic matter. This insatiable commitment to simplification, however, has always been rewarded with the resuscitation of the given object as something new. All traces of superficial or accidental existence are replaced by a complementary value: scintillating symbolic existence.*[3]

Joseph Rykwert in *On Adam's House in Paradise* emphasizes the connection between the elemental in design and the spiritual and religious associations of that architecture.[4] Shinohara seizes this important combination of elemental and spiritual when he writes: "I cannot deny that the quietistic structure of traditional Japanese architecture has found its way into my expression of the eternal elements. I determined that symbolic space was the nucleus of the beautiful spatial tradition of Japan. I ought to express my conception. I create negative space as a protest against frenzied movement about me."[5]

The prototypes for these symbolic spaces are sometimes appropriated by Shinohara from traditional architecture, but are always refigured. In the House of Earth (1966) he exposes the earth in the interior. The ensemble of a floor of clay, lime, and salt, used in conjunction with a hovering roof and distorted square plan, is reminiscent of a farmhouse. Again in the Tanikawa Residence (1974), the earth floor is formed by retaining the slope to reveal the connection between the house and terrain, nature and artifice. Further, the earth floor is used to recall the *doma* in rural buildings of the past *(31)*. Shinohara writes: "In discussing architecture, we may take the *doma* as the point of departure. The *doma* represents the quintessential aspect of a traditional rural dwelling. In this dimly lit simple frame of space, one finds a direct descendant of the dark interiors of the Jomon period dugouts."[6]

31. *Kazuo Shinohara, Tanikawa Residence, 1974*

The sloping dirt floor, the sharply inclined barn-like roof, and the prominence of strong structure in the Tanikawa Residence outline the generic house of some distant past. Shinohara pursues the formal economy of the Zen temple by dismantling past meanings and functions and breathing new life into spaces rendered as negative, "naked" or zero spaces in his attempts to parallel the traditional primitivizing processes of distillation and simplification. On the other hand, such spaces are also his way of frustrating the logic of consumption that seizes the economically rebounding Japan. The rawness of many of his houses (concrete and wood are used in their rough state), in addition to the spareness and strength of structural elements, undermines the pleasure of the house as an object or commodity. While Shinohara rejects any possible resuscitation of meaning from traditional architecture, he cannot let go of the prospect of addressing the issue of meaning and symbolism evoked by these new "naked" spaces. Such meanings, however, require the use of a stochastic method, which he admits implicitly by saying:

Since I do not believe in the existence of total meaninglessness, I am convinced that a relative value can be achieved from elements that have lost meaning and have been reduced to the zero degree, presupposing a context in which meaning was eliminated from symbolic space. I do not plan to return along the path I have trodden but to start again in a new direction. My destination is a primary space, a functional space.[7]

This repeated exposure of space, materials, and elements is molded by French post-war philosophy. The notion of "zero space" is borrowed from Roland Barthes who elaborates the idea in *Writing Degree Zero*.[8] Central to Shinohara's theory is also the use of the structuralism of Claude Lévi-Strauss who affirms the will of all humans to symbolize. Structuralism, moreover, offers a methodology, a strategy of processing the program, site, and structural concerns that again direct him towards those primary, functional spaces. In 1976, he wrote about the influence of Lévi-Strauss:

Although at present I am basically concerned with the expression of things in naked states, suppressing the emergence of meanings, in spite of my wish to do so I still have to find a certain method for fixing aggregations of such things. Consequently, an inclination to move in the direction of unified structures seems to be emerging. I call this contradictory situation "savagery" in analogy with the Pensée Sauvage *of the cultural anthropologist Claude Lévi-Strauss.[9]*

Shinohara's interest in "savagery" is first explored in the House in Uehara of 1976. The model made for the house recalled for him both a Japanese farmhouse with its tangle of beams and studs, and a "jungle." The range of design problems: narrow site, height limitations, building codes, and a crowded program forced several diverging spatial configurations, not always in harmony *(32)*. He wrote about the process:

32. *Kazuo Shinohara, House in Uehara, Tokyo, 1976*

I think this method of dealing directly with the objects themselves may have set my mind to thinking about savagery, though I hasten to add that it was not the idea of savagery that led to the jungle-like appearance. In discussing the thought processes of savages, the noted cultural anthropologist Lévi-Strauss wrote that "each choice which is made will involve a complete reorganization of the structure which will never be the same as one vaguely imagined nor as some other which might have been pre-

44

ferred to it." Though this was not written about architecture, it is a clear expression of how specific decisions, taken one by one, leave their impression on the total concept or the total space.[10]

For Shinohara, it is not the formal associations of savagery that are primary, though there is also a residual fascination with the look of the jungle and its aggregating overgrowth. Rather, the savagery of structural anthropology becomes the means of returning to a conceptual beginning. In structuralism the governing "deep laws" are universal, embedded in the collective mind and transcending any particular culture. Lévi-Strauss suggested that such "structures" were rooted in the functions of the human brain and that it is the mapping of the nexus of relationships and oppositions that determines the dynamic and subject of all arts. Shinohara releases these relations by allowing various properties around each function to emerge and coagulate.[11] The "naked" spaces stripped of all prior meanings and associations become "symbolic" once they realize their various roles in the house.

Predetermination cannot assure a particular clustering of forms, and so, as in the most advanced machines of today, such as the Tom Cat, or moon-landing module, and in nature itself, order is composite, aggravated, and even messy. The House in Uehara is the first step in Shinohara's "savage" journey. A collection of solutions, the house has an uneasy energy. The structure—a complex of vertical supports with 45° braces—has a rude order of its own; as it is shaped by seismic concerns and height limitations, it forces a non-axial circulation. Because the third floor was requested by the client only after the construction had begun, the first two floors have an order that does not recognize the structure or the volume above. The dis-harmony of parts creates an energetic exterior, not easily predicted from the parts. Moreover, the building has an evocative primal power that is partly the shaman's, partly the robot's.

Despite the emphasis on the structural basis of "savagery," Shinohara's work increasingly celebrates the jungle image, if the savage and jungle can be related to a type of agitated, chaotic energy. Shinohara has traveled throughout Africa, yet repeatedly denies any overt connection to the African landscape in his utilization of "savagery" as a concept, claiming that parts of Tokyo were more "jungle-like" (overgrowth, multiple orders, density) than Africa. Such a quality, exacted in increasingly hi-tech materials, can be seen in his work of the 1980s.

Sometimes referred to as "progressive anarchy," the characteristic of his "second machine," derived not from the whole but from the demands of the parts, reenacts jungle associations. The fissure—the symbolic chasm in the spread space pared to essentials in his work of the 1970s—is now excluded. The thicket of functions can be seen in the Tokyo Institute of Technology Centennial Building (1987), where the semi-cylindrical section of lounge and bar invades the body of a building itself subdivided and overcome by circulation and diverse exhibition and lecture spaces. This building is presented not only in the evenly delineated drawings of the 1970s but also in a computer-generated perspective that fully renders the complexity of the solution. Rustic retreats of the 1960s are replaced by the primal order of the future. The symbolism of the 1960s and 1970s which was represented by the void at the core of each building has not been totally eliminated. In the 1980s, the symbolic has been overlaid and amassed in a cacophony of representations.

Hiroshi Hara does not concentrate on the notion of "savagery," but investigates another of Lévi-Strauss' constructs—bricolage. Bricolage, for Hara, is a collage—the combination of quoted elements to create a metaphor. Such metaphors are central to his architecture and the creation of "scenes." These scenes are not entirely concrete or objective allusions. Mood is always the lens to any scene. In his characterization of contemporary architecture in his new manifesto, "Modality," he stresses the necessity for architects to "peep into consciousness" in order to overcome modernism's dependence on function.[12] Such "peeps into consciousness" become the foundations of these "scenes," which are dramatic reinterpretations of the world where the image of nature, a nature of *topos* and climate, is at once amorphous and ambiguous. Such tales can only be retold by the bricoleur.

The paths and boundaries of these scenic realms figure in Hara's own work. His earlier preoccupation with African and Arab settlements focused on the proliferation of orders, textures, and imagery. These habitats provided him with the basic vocabulary which he would use in his early houses. In his own house of 1974, Hara combined the idea of "burying the city within the house"—the structure of the city with its paths and boundaries—with the experience of the natural. The explosion of paths, interchanges and intersections, or the metaphor of settlement, however, is not suggested by the rustic wooden exterior container of his house. Clouds and the fragility of sky are affected by the interior rounded skylights and the introduction of natural light from above *(13)*.

Later projects of Hara develop such scenes by placing more emphasis on the natural narrative. Hi-tech materials, such as metals, reflecting tiles, polished stone, and glass are exploited for their ability to de-materialize, becoming foils to changing light, climate and context. The recent Iida City Museum (1988) and Yamato International Building (1987) in Tokyo appear to be cities of and in the air. They at once recall the ancient hilltown dwellings in Turkey that are close to the clouds, and cloud-like in formation. Primitivism is implied by the cosmogonic reflex to evoke the consciousness of the beginning. "Naturalism" is reconstituted as a mood mediated by a hyper-philosophical understanding, and is engineered in the repeated scenographic vignettes. The imagery is unmistakable without necessarily being identifiable *(33)*.

33. *Hiroshi Hara, Yamato International Building, Tokyo, 1987*

34. *Tadao Ando, row house, Sumiyoshi, Osaka, 1976*

While Ando discusses the notion of *assemblage*, his use of primitivism is, in fact, closer to that of the early modernists. Assemblage emerges, Ando claims, from the traditional *sukiya* house where the importance of the lateral screen-wall system and its revelation of "scene" after scene takes place. He says, "the *sukiya* tradition takes the loose natural scene and recreates it artificially in a tense composition."[13] He is explicit in his admiration of the traditional *sukiya* house and its tie to nature, a nature that has been eclipsed in modern Japan. Discussing nature, he observes: "According to the traditional Japanese interpretation, architecture is always one with nature and attempts to isolate and fix in a point of time nature as it exists in its organic metamorphoses. In other words, it is an architecture reduced to the extremes of simplicity and an aesthetic so devoid of actuality and attributes that it approached theories of *mu*, or nothingness."[14] In contrast to Hara, Ito and Hasegawa, Ando's work, while registering the missing dimension of nature, does not compensate by becoming scenographic *(11, 34)*.

And so, in the spirit of Adorno's *Negative Dialectics*, consumption must be frustrated—an impossibility but nevertheless an objective. While Ando got his start designing high-fashion boutiques and showrooms for the fashion industry, his work has attempted to evade fashion. In the tradition of Brecht, this is an architecture that appears functional but frustrates function and brings into question issues of structure and representation. Ando strives for an aesthetic of discomfort and primitive selectiveness. Kenneth Frampton writes: "In Ando's case, this resistance is predicated on emphasizing the boundary, thereby creating an introspective domain within which the homeowner may be granted sufficient private 'ground' with which to withstand the alienating no-man's land of the contemporary city." He continues to point out the enveloping of a "primitive space."[15]

The absence of that nature must be made present and becomes a subtext to Ando's constructions. Ando achieves this by the use of walls, in the modern material, concrete. The closure, his walls' effect, have been well analyzed in their ability to exclude the urban chaos and to create a preserve of space. He says explicitly that he has attempted to "project a primitive image scene inside the territory delineated by the walls in this house" *(35)*.[16]

In "A Wedge in Circumstance," Ando characterizes his work: "First, I use limited materials and expose their characteristic textures. Second, my spaces are not always given clear functional articulation. I believe that these characteristics most effectively enable me to produce spatial prototypes. The strong nuances of simple materials and their textures emphasize simple spatial compositions, and in this way provoke an awareness of a dialogue with natural elements such as light and wind." He goes on to say that his reason for adopting this method is related "to the desire to inspire internal vistas within the individual and to correspond to spaces that the individual harbors within himself. For this reason, I emphasize the indefinite parts related to human emotion and to the interstitial zones between functionally established spaces. I call this spatial prototype the sentiment-fundamental space. Once it has been created, I follow this procedure to sublimate it into a symbolic space."[17]

Similarly to the preceding architects, Toyo Ito begins his symbolic quest with primitivism. His earlier houses explored the "archaeological" origins of architecture. The U-House in Nakano (1976) was both cavern-like, with its piercing introduction of top-light, and organic, resembling an atectonic intestine *(12, 36)*. Ito

35. *Tadao Ando, Wall House, Ashiya, 1981*

37. *Toyo Ito, House in Magomezawa, Funabashi, 1986*

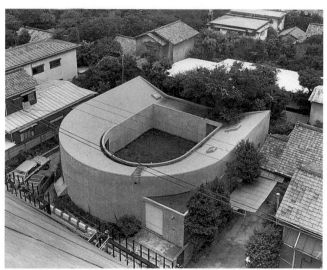

36. *Toyo Ito, U-House, Nakano, Tokyo, 1976*

writes of his Y-Court House with its trabeated pergola that, "in terms of composition, it is the most primitive type in which relations among architectural elements can be compared."[18] In the Silver Hut (1984), Ito begins an exploration of "anemorphic" (wind) architecture, continuing the anti-formal, symbolic explorations of Hara and Shinohara. Forms deformed by the wind allude to an architecture of change. An alternative primitive order eclipses rationality, hierarchy and limits as well as evades the bounds of Western classical philosophy and mathematics.

Ito borrows the concept of "nomadism" from Gilles Deleuze and Felix Guattari who depict another migratory beginning in *Mille Plateaux*. The fundamental difference in their primitive model is the notion of the nomadic, as opposed to the sedentary, which completely determines order, knowledge, and occupation. Western metaphysics based on authority and complicity with the state is denounced in favor of the forces of nature, change and the open-ended traversing of space. Nomadic space is unwritten and undesigned—smooth.[19] The appearance of architecture is related to the birth of the "first city." Through the notion of de-territorialization, the last connection to past architecture could be broken. Architecture would be severed from the site *(37)*.

Ito, recasts what are offered as icons of this "other" order. His *pao* project, Dwelling for the Tokyo Nomad Woman of 1985, an installation for a department store, updates the nomad's baggage and makes clear that this baggage is a substitute for the house. Ironically, under Ito's gaze, survival in the present takes on an incidental quality. Survival is not really in the hands of any ordinary man or woman, and so "survival" and "shelter" are seen in all their contemporary superficiality. The dwelling of the Tokyo Nomad Woman accommodates grooming, snacking, and entertainment. The aims of present society are acknowledged.

In the Nomad Club (1986), a temporary restaurant

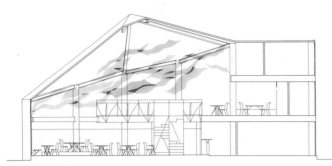

38. *Toyo Ito, Nomad Club, Tokyo, 1986*

in Roppongi, Ito makes the analogy between contemporary urbanites and nomads: "The restaurant serves as an oasis for the adventurers who enjoy life as their fancy goes and travel in cities . . . an image of a huge tent briefly encamped in the desert of the city, glittering with neon-like stars in the sky" *(38)*.[20] Mirage-like, the glittering and transparent interior conforms to any dictum. Furnished with light, soft, mobile and fragmented objects, the interior meets a variety of needs with a limited repertoire of pieces. The fittings of nomadic life are suggested by the tent-like superstructure (temporary, conforming to site and terrain) and the furnishings, which are infinitely adaptable. The construction methods and materials are far from rustic. Perforated aluminum, expanded metals, custom-made steel frames, and connections of complex design are specified in these projects.

His Tower of Winds in Yokohama (1986) dramatizes the natural wind through de-naturalized technology. Perforated metal screens cover a ventilation tower wrapped in acrylic mirrored plates. Thousands of electric bulbs are arranged between the screens and the tower, programmed by a computer to register the variations in the wind and communicate that change through patterns of light and sound.

Both the Sports Complex in Owani (1985) and the project for the Fujisawa Municipal Cultural Complex (1986) appear to be high-tech camping. Reflective metallic materials—glass domes in the Fujisawa project, and wooden trusses covered with fiberglass fabric coated with Teflon in Owani—suggest impermanence and a connection to the elements. Ito writes about the Fujisawa project: "This plan proposes the whole structure to be collapsible like tents in a bazaar in Islamic countries. This is a protest against public buildings which are reduced to corpses of modernism corrupted by authoritarianism."[21] The stadium and cultural center are not easily demountable.

The analogy of the nomadic tent allows us to ponder an architecture that is tempered by climate—often ignored because modern technology's capacity to moderate the effects of climate is so accepted. Ito's critique of modern life as a vacuum forced by the sociology of rapid change and modernization can be appreciated as a text, but his approach to textuality is classical. A story is told through spatial forms (now light) that represent and have

meaning in a signifier-to-signified relationship. In contrast, post-structuralism advocates the free flow of meanings and signs to generate dissemination and new contents, engendering complete metamorphosis. Ito's earlier PMT building, with its peeling façade, came closer to the notion of Deleuze and Guattari's "diagrammatic sign" in its capacity to map contradictory fluxes of energies and meanings.

Itsuko Hasegawa, also a disciple of Shinohara, shares with Hara and Ito an obsession with the loss of a natural center and an attempt to translate the core of the symbolic in traditional Japanese architecture. In her description of Work M, subtitled *Natural Scenery, Analogy of Nature*, she objectifies her task:

It seems that deep down in their longings, there exists an ideal of Japanese people that has been fostered throughout the long history of an agricultural society. It must be a kind of natural scenery with surrounding mountains, flowing rivers, weep of rice paddies, lakes and oceans, and scattered houses, shrines, and temples. Various architectural symbols of Western and Japanese origin are arranged in typical commercialized houses, but I attempt to trap natural scenery by using symbols analogous to nature. The stretch of small roofs arranged around the surroundings brings the image of the mountains. Mountains and a sea of trees stand like a shadow picture on the vertical surface. What is expressed here might be a kind of utopian fiction, but I think it can also be regarded as a natural scenery of the future for the new generation.[22]

In her designs, Hasegawa choreographs the natural, introducing light, wind, and landscape through a variety of techniques. She creates landscapes within and with her buildings—landscapes that reflect the continuity of many of Shinohara's preoccupations. She assembles her forms like a bricoleur. Her spaces reject the denial, the quest for the zero space of Shinohara's earlier work, but her landscapes attempt to charge architecture with the power of a symbolic landscape. Like Lévi-Strauss' "savage," her will is to symbolize. About Bizan Hall, Hasegawa weaves the following fairy tale:

The pyramids located in the courtyard for lighting and ventilation of the Large Room, made of aluminum punched metal and glass, seem objects that combine the images of some ancient landscape, the sun god and a futuristic space station. It is a poetic machine echoing the call of the ancient past, the distant future . . . all these roofs, superimposed over one another, look like a sea of trees, or a range of mountains, appealing to the visitor as a group of analogical symbols of nature (39).[23]

In criticism of Hasegawa's work and in her own words, her role as a woman, as an "other," is deliberated. Her self-perceived "marginality" makes her acutely sensitive to the realm of the primitive—the "others" excluded, though not in any direct polemic. She says about her work: "It is essentially a feminine discourse . . . from which meaninglessness and multiple meaning would

39. Itsuko Hasegawa, Bizan Hall, Shizuoka City, 1984

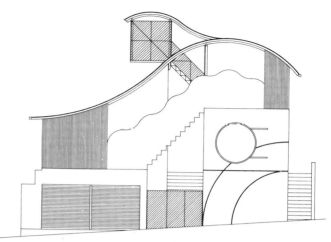

40. Itsuko Hasegawa, House in Nerima, Tokyo, 1986

gush forward."[24] This feminine discourse has been recognized if not exactly identified. Critics of her work regularly applaud her liberating methodology and metaphors without associating them with that realm of "otherness." *Childlike, intuitive, instinctive,* and *nonrational* are adjectives often attributed to her works. Hajime Yatsuka writes about Hasegawa's Fujisawa Cultural Center that "it is like a fairy tale village on the moon out of a children's book."[25] Koji Taki dwells on Hasegawa's "instinctive creation of architecture" and the "unconscious elements" that are always in her architecture. Hiroyuki Suzuki examines the mediating of the "paternal" spaces that perhaps originate in the works of Hasegawa's symbolic father, Shinohara.[26] On two levels, then, Hasegawa has critically capitalized on the primitive in her architecture. By re-formulating a panoply of shifting primal landscapes from the outside, she has, both as a modernist and post-structuralist primitive, internally and externally realized a new origin *(19, 40).*

Yasumitsu Matsunaga's most recent works examine the cross currents of post-structuralist philosophy. In a residence in Tsukuba called Inscription he plays not only with the origins of architecture, knowledge, and life, but also with the acceptance of the impossibility of ever knowing about these beginnings. Following the lead of Daedalus, Leonardo da Vinci and Vladimir Tatlin (who spent ten years inaugurating his flying machine, the Letatlin), Matsunaga brings to his design an understanding of the demands of gravity and its defiance in buildings. From the first lines of "Into the Height of the Sky," an essay written in 1987, he establishes: "The origin of the universe; that of the life; that of the mind: these three are deemed to be eternally unsolvable enigmas."[27] He goes on to outline the attempts of European philosophers to come to terms with these enigmas. Architecture's "loss of center" is the result of post-structuralist critiques. Limits and rationality are also the victims of these meanderings. Thus, the "fractal landscape" cultivated in the Inscription house earth-work (indebted to Richard Serra

for its title) is "derived from a resolute intention to imitate...nature [by] introducing random digit systems."[28] Matsunaga maintains that such a landscape "could never become chaos itself." The architecture and garden are of a revealed nature. Inscription resembles a primal bird, a dodo landed on a prehistoric or pre-Euclidean landscape. The power of the interior spaces and cluster of buildings comes from its relation to the ground—struggle for dominance savored from the interior and exterior.

Yasumitsu Matsunaga's reevaluation of nature shares characteristics with some of Toyo Ito's, Hiroshi Hara's and Itsuko Hasegawa's landscapes. In the Daita Housing Project (1989), Matsunaga attempts to generate a cosmic model *(20, 41).* "It is just a coincidence," he writes, "that the configuration reminds one of the model of the bubble-like structure of the universe which the latest cosmic theory has verified."[29] This latest and "futuristic" cosmic model also replicates more basic, "primitive" forms. Matsunaga acknowledges this when he writes:

Architecture could also be considered as a kind of shelter standing on this planet to protect people for the weight of the universe with a depth of 15 billion light-years. This fact is true without any discrimination, with the tents in the deserts as well as with the skyscrapers in the cities. When you visit an Islamic city like Isfahan, you will notice that everything including markets, mosques, or houses is uniformly covered by a series of domes undulating like a sheet of veil. This might have come from Islamic philosophy formulated by the recognition of the space of the desert extending infinitely between heaven and the earth. It might have sensed intuitively that from the viewpoint of the God, namely from the universe, no difference among human activities could be noticed, and everything could be covered under a soft sheet of shelter.[30]

In one of his latest houses, the T-House in Higashi-Kurume, Tokyo, Matsunaga says that he has produced a house that is peculiar and resembles at once a bird or

42. *Riken Yamamoto, Gazebo Building, Yokohama, 1986*

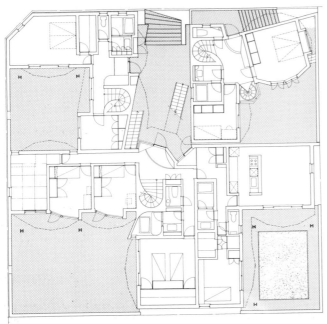

41. *Yasumitsu Matsunaga, Daita Housing Project, Tokyo, 1989*

(first floor plan, above; axonometric, below)

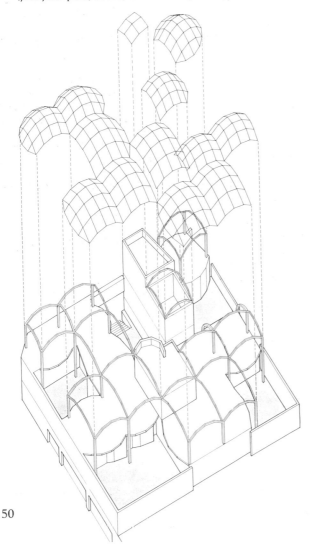

butterfly from the outside, with an interior of womb-like space. This house, as in Inscription, pursues simultaneously a "totem-like" primitivism and a universalizing *topos*. The house, he says, is "appropriate as an 'imago mundi,'" as it contains a sun, moon, and stars.[31]

This fascination with the primal *topos* is extended in the work of Riken Yamamoto. The Hamlet project of 1988, as well as his earlier projects, reflects, as do works of Hara, his study of settlements in undeveloped countries. In projects such as the Gazebo (1986) and Rotunda (1987), a base gives rise to villages that are both tented and domed *(21, 42)*. In Hamlet, four families share a complex that Yamamoto characterizes as a highrise canyon under a huge translucent tent of Teflon. He writes: "The inhabitants of this new structure now live in a highrise canyon; almost totally isolated ... this new home is like a besieged hamlet where those who have chosen to live together in the city are making their last stand."[32]

Kazuyo Sejima approaches the creation of "smooth" space—a limitless, fluid *topos*—in her Platform buildings (1988) *(43)*. She says that she is attempting to develop a "limitlessly stretchable place and a cover that does not determine actions. For this, a series of two L-shaped frames is built with a thin, undulating roof cover, which emerges like a never-ending pattern. While the wave-like roof covers the actions occurring underneath, these actions could stretch forward by crossing the frames."[33] Prodding the static status of architecture, Sejima asserts that architecture must be related to action. This action is episodic rather than sequential—a traditional notion of time in narrative that circumscribes narratives in novels and film in Japan. She writes that she considers architecture as "a site or locale where a number of actions can pass by. Could architecture be a temporary phenomenon that appears in an action-maker's awareness as images when actions move across the locale?"[34] Both time and place have been relativized in the smooth flux of architecture. The interplay of time and space approaches both the ancient notion of *ma* and Einstein's relativity, so that the past, present and future close in on one another.

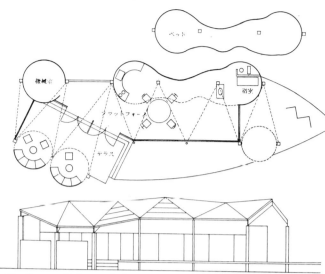

43. *Kazuyo Sejima, Platform No. 2 House (plan, top; elevation, above)*

44. *Ryoji Suzuki, House in Kigashi-kurume, 1985*

Sejima and architects such as Ryoji Suzuki extend post-structuralist re-visions of time and *topos* to architecture. Suzuki, in his architecture, creates territories of discovery *(44)*. They are like Ozu's films, he says, without plots but with the pulp of tension.[35] Such explorations appear to produce provocative buildings, even if the texts become increasingly hermetic. The initial impulse of Shinohara and his disciples, to maintain something of the primal power of Japanese architecture in the complicated present, remains for the future. Folded, subverted, and superposed by post-structuralism, the present and past persist, assembled as material for the present generation of Japanese architects.

NOTES

1. Rosalind Krauss, "No More Play," *The Originality of the Avant-Garde and Other Modernist Myths* (Cambridge: MIT Press, 1986), p. 52. An excellent discussion of the use of primitive art by Giacometti, Alberto, and others in the early decades of the 20th century.

2. See Kenneth Frampton's article "Towards a Critical Regionalism," in Hal Foster, ed. *The Anti-Aesthetic* (Port Townsend: Bay Press, 1983), where he discusses the universalizing tendencies of modernism.

3. Kazuo Shinohara in *Shinohara, IAUS 17* (New York: Rizzoli, 1982), p. 115.

4. Joseph Rykwert, *On Adam's House in Paradise: The Idea of the Primitive Hut in Architectural History* (Cambridge: MIT Press, 1981).

5. Kazuo Shinohara, *11 Houses and Architectural Theory*, Vol. 2 (Tokyo: Bijutsu Shuppan-sha, 1976).

6. Shinohara, op. cit., 3, p. 115.

7. Ibid, p. 15.

8. Roland Barthes, *Writing Degree Zero* (New York: Hill and Wang, 1968). Trans. A. Lavers and C. Smith.

9. *Shinohara*, Societé Française des Architectes (SADG) (Paris, 1980), also quoted in Yasumitsu Matsunaga, "Architecture as Text: Kazuo Shinohara in his Third Phase," *Shinohara*, op. cit., 3, p. 8.

10. Ibid.

11. Here the term *function* is used, as always with Shinohara, in a very broad and anti-modernist manner.

12. Hiroshi Hara, "Modality—Central Concept of Contemporary Architecture," *Japan Architect* (November/December, 1986), p. 24.

13. Tadao Ando, "From Self-Enclosed Modern Architecture Towards Universality," in Kenneth Frampton, ed., *Tadao Ando: Buildings, Projects, Writings* (New York: Rizzoli, 1984), p. 140.

14. Ibid.

15. Frampton, "Tadao Ando's Critical Modernism," op. cit., 13, p. 6.

16. Frampton, op. cit., 13, p. 129.

17. Ando, "A Wedge in Circumstances," op. cit., 13, p. 134.

18. See my discussion of Ito's U-House and Silver Hut in "Ito and Ecriture," *Space Design* (September, 1986), p. 90. The 'Y-Court House' is a project Ito prepared for a design conference in New York, 1982.

19. Hajime Yatsuka, in his article "Between Deconstruction and Nomadism" (unpublished paper), discussed many of these points in detail.

20. Toyo Ito, "Project for the Restaurant 'Nomad' (1986)" *Space Design* (September, 1986), p. 32.

21. Ito, "Project for Fujisawa Municipal Cultural Complex (1986)," ibid, p. 29.

22. Itsuko Hasegawa, *Space Design* (April, 1985), p. 12.

23. Ibid, p. 57.

24. Ibid, p. 108.

25. Hajime Yatsuka, "An Architecture Floating on the Sea of Signs," *Architectural Design: Japanese Architecture* (Vol. 58, No. 5/6, 1988), p. 10.

26. Op. cit., 22.

27. Yasumitsu Matsunaga, "Into the Height of the Sky," *Kenchiku Bunka* (November, 1987), p. 108.

28. Ibid, p. 109.

29. Unpublished paper.

30. Ibid.

31. Ibid.

32. Riken Yamamoto, "A Hamlet in the City," *Japan Architect* (January, 1989), p. 45.

33. Kazuyo Sejima, "Platform No. 1, Katsuura, 1988." See in this volume.

34. Ibid.

35. Ryoji Suzuki, "The Moment of 'Eureka': Concerning 'Experience in Material,'" *Japan Architect* (August, 1988), p. 60.

THE ARCHITECTS

ARATA ISOZAKI

Tsukuba Center Building • Tsukuba • 1983

If I were to say that this building is the expression of the absence of something, I might not be taken seriously. Yet, the central concept of the design is that very absence. Visually there is a clearly defined center. In such a center one would expect to find a symbol of authority of exalted position—of majesty, officialdom, the state or the sovereign. But what happens if you choose a method that omits that expected presence? This design is the result of my experimentation with just such an idle question.

When you visit the building you will come upon the oval-shaped, sunken plaza. Yet, rather than descending directly to the lower level, you gaze around at the hotel on the east side, and at the facade of the concert hall on the south side. You might find yourself wandering into these buildings, but nothing attracts you to descend to the oval plaza. Right below you is the focal point; oriented toward it are two water sources and these two streams meet and are drawn into one stream that disappears into the earth.

Although situated just as the Campidoglio with its crowning statue of Marcus Aurelius, in this design every relationship is reversed: this square is the lowest point in the whole. If there is any ruling concept, it lies in this central point, and it is the point where one would expect to be given visualized substance, for this becomes the center of sight. But it is also here that the structure of the design has undergone an inversion process. In the Tsukuba Center Building, I randomly scattered design elements borrowed from my close friends and many of my respected predecessors, embedding their distinctive aspects into the whole. This building is a group portrait, so to speak, of architects such as Ledoux, Giulio Romano, Michelangelo, Otto Wagner, Michael

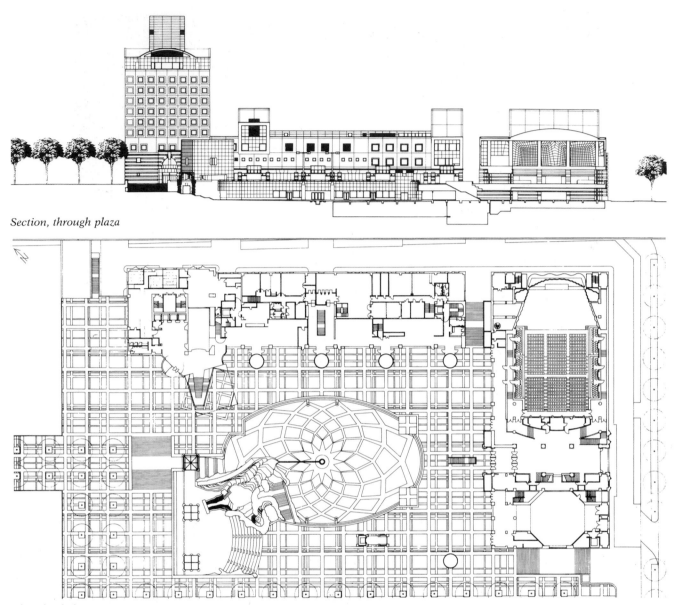

Section, through plaza

Plaza level plan

Graves, Richard Meier, Charles Moore, Aldo Rossi, Hans Hollein, Peter Cook, Adalberto Libera, Philip Johnson, Leon Krier, Lawrence Halprin, Ettore Sottsass, and many more. I introduced clashing and harmonious clusters of these diverse fragments, and for most of the fragments I have cited historical forms. Yet, once borrowed, they are torn out of the context of which they were originally a part and transferred into a newly created context. In the process of transfer, some elements have been greatly changed, some so thoroughly abstracted that they cannot be identified.

This building possesses the complex structure of a long novel, and the reason it is filled with so many direct and quite concrete allusions is to endow the details or fragments with an independent and powerful dynamic of their own. In other words, I had to make each detail self-sustaining so that it could stand without relation to others. But the explicit representation of these concretely manifested fragments is by no means consistent, nor do they converge on one point, but ceaselessly revolve around the periphery of that unoccupied center. If one were to give a metaphor for the void center, it might be that everything—line of vision, water, meaning, representation—is devoured by the earth itself as a result of its own form. *A. Isozaki*

KISHO KUROKAWA

Hiroshima City Museum of Contemporary Art • 1988

The design of the Hiroshima City Museum of Contemporary Art is based on the philosophy of symbiosis. The reappraisal of modernism and modern architecture means the reappraisal of the dominance of the West and the logos which are part and parcel of modernism. The cultural references of postmodern architecture in Europe and the United States are also based in the West and, in that respect, post-modern architecture does not differ from modern architecture. Whether we chose to label it post-modern or neo-modern, the first task facing those who seek to reform modern architecture is to trans-

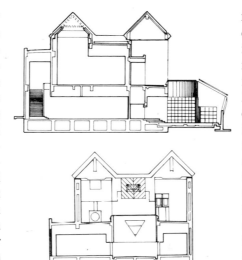

Transverse sections

form the paradigm of Western domination. In this sense, my idea of symbiosis with heterogeneous cultures is one transformation of that paradigm. Moreover, in order to evoke more creative and multivalent meanings, a symbiosis of history and the future, and of historical signs and symbols, must be subjected to transformation, articulation, sophistication, and intermediation. The doctrine of rationalism and the logos of modernism, furthermore, meant that humanity (and architecture) were called on to control and restrain nature, that lay both inside and outside the wildness that is sensitivity.

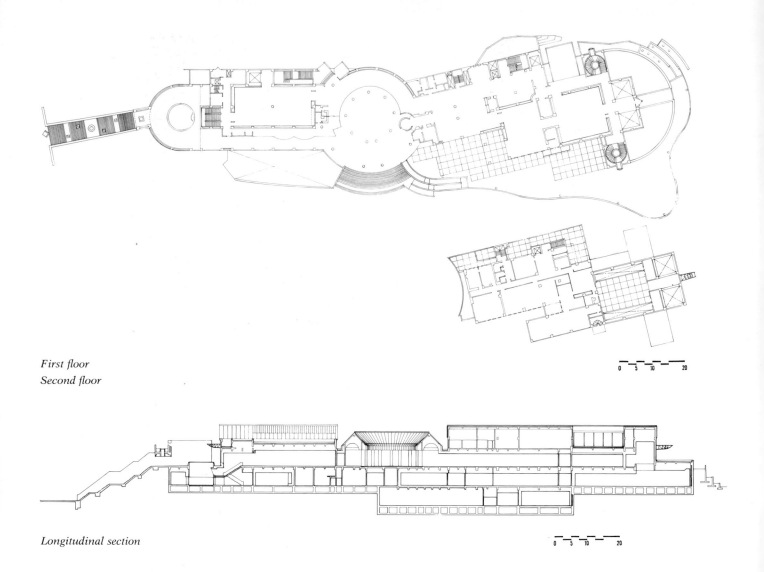

First floor
Second floor

Longitudinal section

The concept of the symbiosis of humanity (architecture) and nature lies in a transformation of the paradigm of the dominance of logos.

The Hiroshima City Museum of Contemporary Art has been carefully situated on the ridge of the Hijiyama hill to give priority, as much as possible, to the preservation of the wooded areas on the slopes of the hill. In order to keep the height of the building from exceeding that of the surrounding trees, part of the exhibition space is set underground; as a result, some 60 percent of the total floor space is below ground. Many intermediary zones between the work of architecture and its natural setting have been incorporated into the building's exterior—an open central plaza with colonnade, a patio, a corridor, a stone garden, a stairway sculpted from stone—facilitating the symbiosis of architecture and nature, interior and exterior. The materials used on the building exterior also evolve gradually, from the natural stone foundation upward to roughly finished stone, polished stone, tile, and aluminum—from earth to sky, from ground to the universe, from the past to the future, all in symbiosis, which is an understanding and a method I have followed for nearly a decade.

The overall shape of the museum is a linked series of gabled

roofs. As they are segmented, they create a work of architecture that is a village, a group of dwellings; we might call this the symbiosis of part and whole. This has permitted the museum to achieve a sense of scale that does not dominate its natural setting. The gabled roofs are a quotation of Edo period earthen storehouses, but the use of the contemporary material, aluminum, transforms that historical sign and imparts it with ambiguity. The central plaza along the main approach is a quotation of a Western city, yet in its center there is no fountain or work of sculpture indicating an empty center or the absence of a center. The roof over the colonnade that surrounds the central plaza is cut away at the front, in the direction that faces the city center, connoting the site of the atomic bombing, and the pillars of the colonnade rise from stones exposed by the blast. Like the *roji* entryway garden leading to a tea room, this approach plaza has no particular function, yet it is an important agent in the evocation of meanings emerging out of the symbiosis of history and the present, as well as of heterogeneous cultures. *K. Kurokawa*

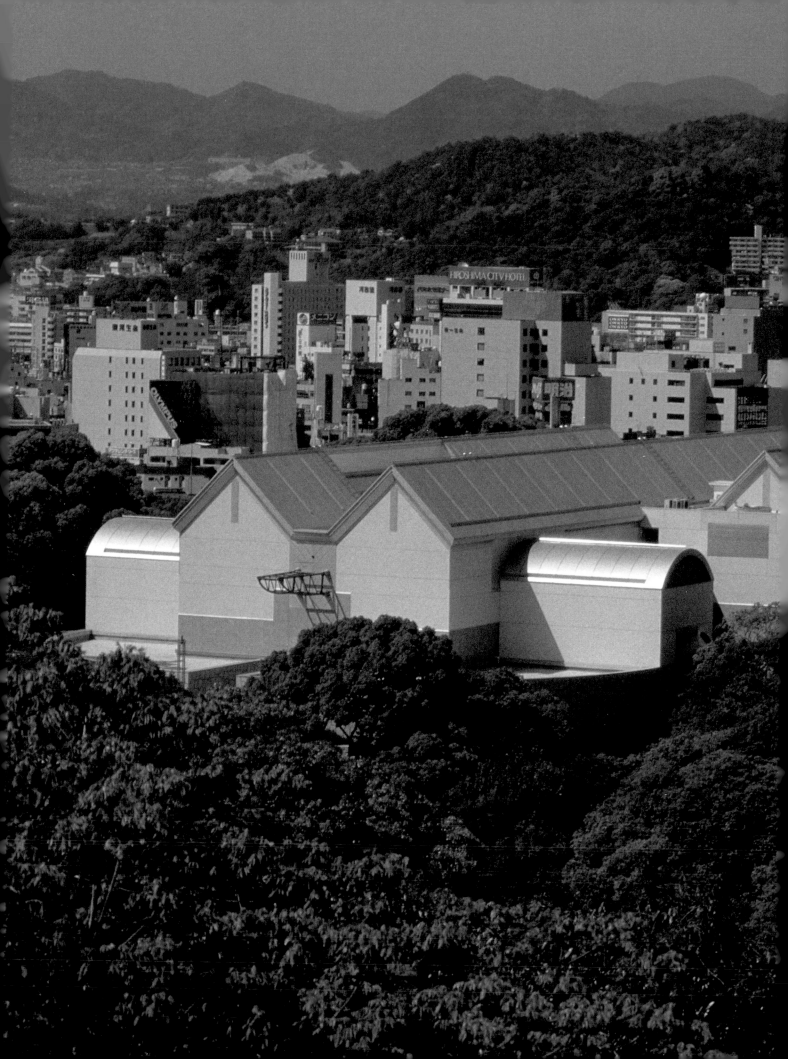

FUMIHIKO MAKI

Spiral • Tokyo • 1985

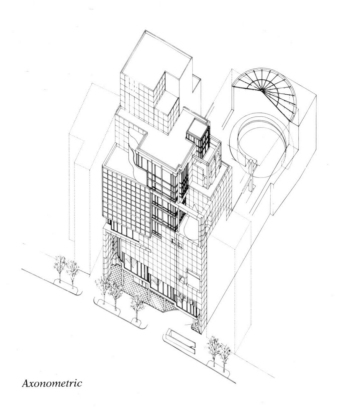

Axonometric

Since World War II, the Wacoal Corporation has grown into one of Japan's largest manufacturers of women's lingerie. In part to improve its corporate image, the company has recently expanded its program to include fashion, art, and music. This building is an active arts center for various corporate-sponsored cultural activities, and must be in itself a work of art.

The first floor, including the entrance lobby, is designed for the display of temporary exhibitions. The main space for these installations is the semi-cylindrical, multi-storied atrium, lit by natural light, in the back of the

building. A cafe is located in the middle of this space and directly below a mezzanine level we call a watchtower. A gently sloping ramp along the curving wall of the atrium leads to a shop of designers' crafts. A visitor may also reach the second floor from what we call the esplanade, if upon entering the building lobby he turns right and continues up a stairway in the direction of the street. The esplanade continues upward through a high-ceilinged space to the third-floor foyer of a theater. The theater, which seats three hundred, will be used for various performances and activities. Video studios are located on the

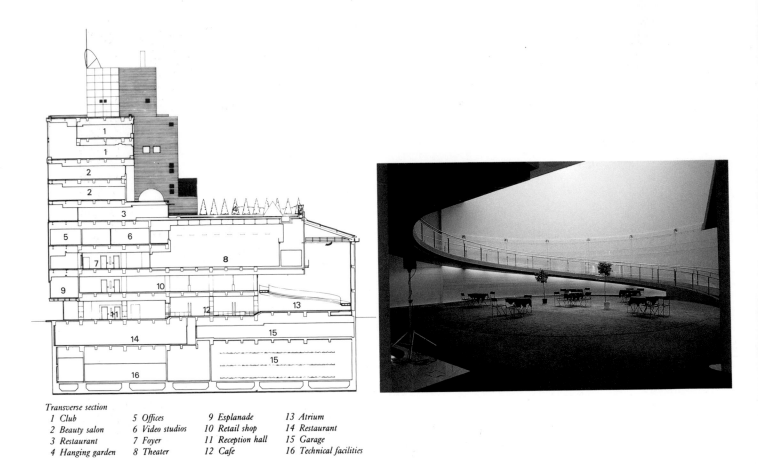

Transverse section

1 Club	5 Offices	9 Esplanade	13 Atrium
2 Beauty salon	6 Video studios	10 Retail shop	14 Restaurant
3 Restaurant	7 Foyer	11 Reception hall	15 Garage
4 Hanging garden	8 Theater	12 Cafe	16 Technical facilities

fourth floor, a restaurant with a garden on the fifth floor. Each of these spaces for art and design-related activities has its own distinctive character. The conical form, which is a particularly striking feature of the elevation, functions as a special exhibition room for a costume museum. The eighth and ninth floors of the Center accommodate the owner's private spaces for entertainment, and various kinds of clubs. This two-story space, which we call an acropolis, has a maisonette arrangement, and will be used for conferences, parties, and small exhibitions; necessary service space has also been provided. The free-form volume houses a bar.

The buildings along Aoyama Boulevard are mostly combinations of rectangular prisms. If the exterior surface of Spiral is

distinctive in this context, it is not because of any unusual imagery but because the building offers images and materials that people are not certain they have seen before.

Creation in architecture is discovery, not invention. It is not a pursuit of something that transcends the imagination but a cultural act in response to the common imagination or vision of the time. However, only a fine and shifting line divides the new from the familiar. The days when there was an immutable style and when there were clearly two distinct types of urban architecture, public and private, are past. In an industrialized society, group imagination manifests itself in unstable and diverse ways.

The classical urban order having collapsed, any work of ar-

chitecture that, in a sense, internalizes the city and functions on its exterior surface as a mechanism of transmission will gradually come to have a public character, no matter how small it is or what explicit function it has.

Spiral symbolizes today's image of the city—an environment that is fragmented but that constantly renews its vitality precisely through its state of fragmentation. It represents an attempt at various levels to achieve goals that were originally modernism's, including a dynamic equilibrium, a vocabulary of masses and volumes, a whole that subsumes conflicting parts, and a system of industrial materials that is made to respond to the architect's sensibility. *F. Maki*

National Museum of Modern Art • Kyoto • 1986

Okazaki Park, located in the northeastern corner of Japan's ancient capital, is the earliest modern park in Japan. The city's major cultural facilities are concentrated here, and the great red *torii* gate leading to Heian Shrine, one of the city's most significant attractions, is a symbol of the park. The area is designated a historic/scenic zone and buildings are limited to 20 meters in height. The museum is the new building for a national collection of twentieth-century Western and Japanese art.

The main entrance to the museum is on the east side facing the approach to Heian Shrine and opens into the first floor lobby. Other spaces on the first floor include a restaurant, a gallery, an auditorium, and a large office. The director's office, a departmental office, and a library are located on the second floor; temporary exhibition galleries are on the third floor; permanent exhibition galleries are on the fourth. The basement level of the museum accommodates storage and mechanical space. The plan is centered around a symbolic, skylit atrium. Most visitors will use the stairway in the atrium to go to the third-floor temporary exhibition space. Stairs are located on three of the four corners of the building. Pushing these vertical circulation spaces (and mechanical spaces) to the corners increases the flexibility of the exhibition spaces on the third and fourth floors. The service spaces are located in the back (i.e., on the west side) of the building. In contrast to the stone and paint of the central staircase, the one in the southeast corner employs a composition of metal and panels. It is designed to generate a DeStijl world by means of the various details and external views visible to people mounting and descending it. Though different in mood, this method, in which scenes develop and details participate according to pre-established leitmotifs, shares something in common with the Spiral Building. *F. Maki*

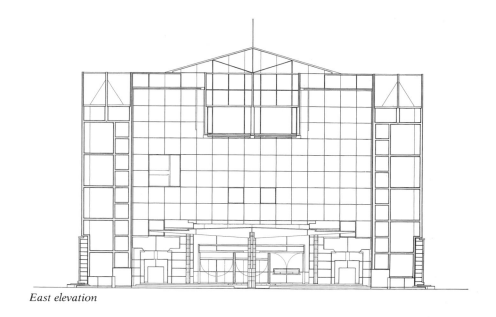

East elevation

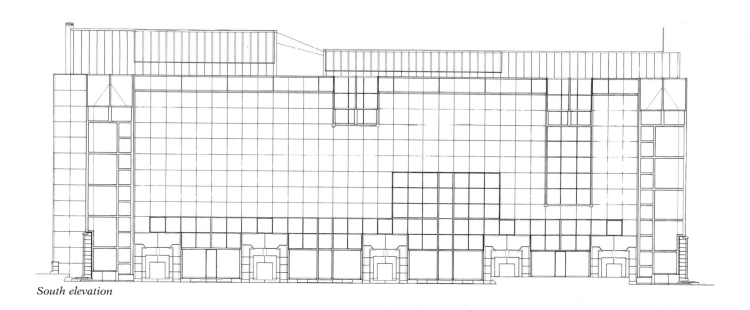

South elevation

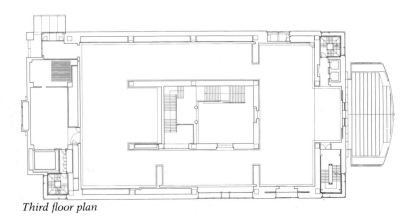

Third floor plan

Site plan showing ground floor plan

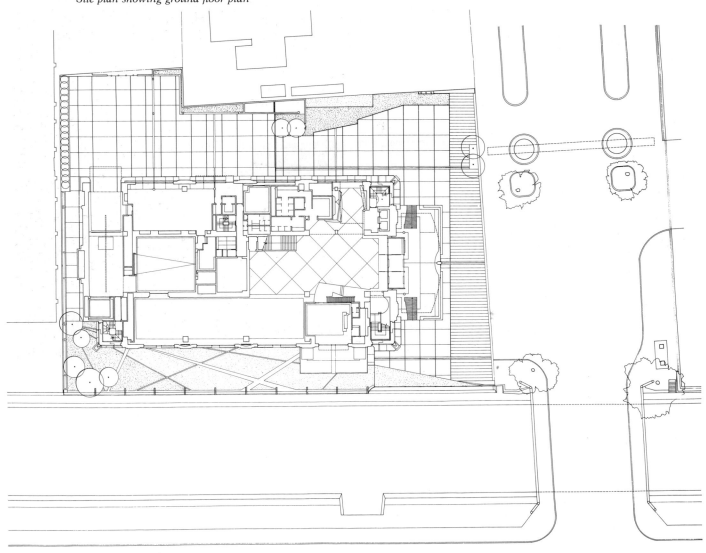

KAZUO SHINOHARA

House in Yokohama • 1984

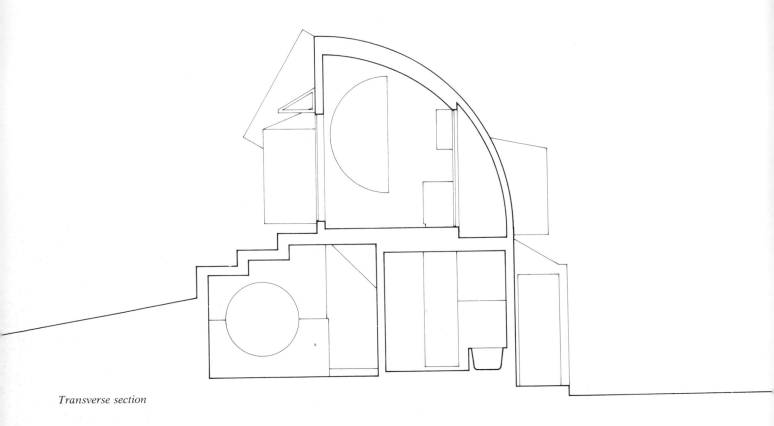

Transverse section

In explaining his work, Shinohara often refers to what he calls the zero-degree machine. His machine, however, differs from that which the modernists idealized in their designs. Shinohara's inspiration comes from such technological advancements of the latter part of this century as, for example, the US Navy's F–14 fighter plane and the Apollo 11 lunar landing craft. Both represent the ultimate in the technologies of their time, yet they exhibit forms of extreme complexity and are devoid of the streamlined formal synthesis the pioneers of modernism were striving for in architecture.

Positioned on a sloping wooded site, Shinohara's own home is attached to an older, traditional house in a way that it respects, as much as possible, the surrounding environment and the existing structure. Yet, the various individual forms and volumes of the new house, all corresponding to different functions, are joined abruptly; they are designed and assembled as parts of a science-fiction machine. By way of this abrupt, though by no means unconditional, mode of integration, generating what Shinohara calls random noise, the house becomes the juxtaposition of spatial units belonging to dif-

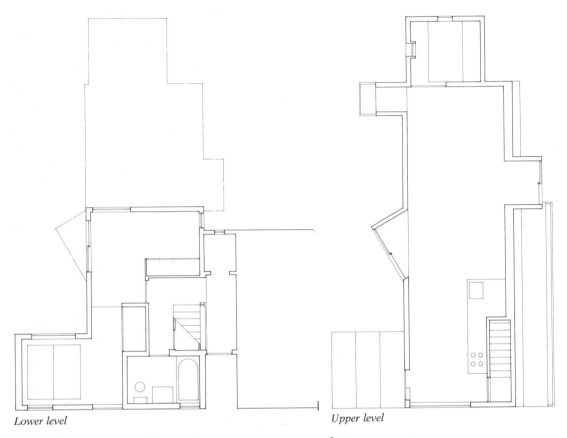

Lower level   Upper level

ferent compositional contexts.

Thus, as Shinohara's designs tend to be, this house, too, is rather highly idiosyncratic, projecting itself out of the raw earth in an aggressive, yet controlled amalgamation of concrete, steel, and corrugated aluminum. The small tatami room with a stepped roof aligns itself in a seemingly illogical manner to the main volume as does the cylindrical space at the rear of the house. Window and door openings take on a variety of geometrical shapes and positions which, with their ambiguous quality, lend themselves to spontaneous human interactions of movement and to the unexpected changes of penetrating light. The quarter-cylinder main volume, while allowing adequate sunlight into the adjacent struc-

ture, promotes a unique dialogue between the pristine white surfaces of its interior, the iconistic furniture, and the randomly framed and fragmented vistas. Relatively uneventful, the entry leads to a flight of stairs where one first catches sight of the cylindrical ceiling. Nevertheless, it is only after turning the corner that the visitor is exposed to the full impact of the stark white interior—a mastery of volumetric space—which, depending on the angle of the sun, can emit a shimmering glow, imbuing at times the experience with a rare feeling of surreality. Yet, the effect is also one of serenity and reverberation, a sense of interaction with the natural surrounding that transcends the conventional. *Keith Krolak*

"There exists in Tokyo," says Kazuo Shinohara, "a complete antithesis of the beautiful and orderly urban compositions found in the West." By recognizing, though not necessarily endorsing this chaotic urban situation, Shinohara has been, for quite some time, pursuing the concept of "progressive anarchy" as the focus of design in his architecture. This pursuit, which runs parallel with his striving for a "zero-degree machine," characterizes his recent works exceptionally well, but none more so than the Centennial Hall of the Tokyo Institute of Technology.

Shinohara has landed this latest building machine of his at the entrance of the campus with such mind-boggling intensity that it not only responds to, but in fact, decidedly transcends the urban energy and vitality found outside the university gates. Apparently, the architectural approach in relation to the built environment has been derived from "the fearsome super-technology contained in [the] elements and apparatuses and [their] relationships established inside" such products as an F–14 fighter plane or the Apollo lunar module, the new fascinations of Shinohara.

By juxtaposing an inverted half-cylinder and a rectangular parallelepiped, the basic image of the building was established—a "shining cylinder, floating in the air." Achieving this, however, through a *sachlich* or extraordi-nary connections in a country plagued with earthquakes, required the talents of Toshihiko Kimura, Shinohara's structural consultant since the mid–1960s. He treated the cylindrical form as a beam structure that interlocks with the vertical legs of the parallelepiped. During the design process, the axis of the half-cylinder was bent, now thrusting out towards the local train station on the east while making similar gestures toward the central campus on the western end.

This stainless-steel-clad inverted cylinder, containing the restaurant/bar and lounge, and from where distant views of Mount Fuji are afforded on clear days, can thus be interpreted in several ways. One could recognize the architect's intent to establish dialogues between campus and city, form and structure, technology and nature, and so on.

Perhaps more dramatic is another metaphor, that of the fuselage of some giant aircraft piercing the entire conference area; that is both awesome and kinetic.

Gallery areas in the double-height entrance hall and in the basement are characteristically austere but not simplistic; they are intentionally discrete but not neutral. In spite of their geometrical tension through the marriage of massive walls to glazed openings, and the stoic, sculptural accent of the staircase, these spaces can also highlight what is being exhibited in them.

Proclaimed by Shinohara as a product of his fourth stage in design, the Centennial Hall bears solemn yet dramatic testimony to his quest for "the conditions of space that will characterize architecture and cities in the future." *Keith Krolak*

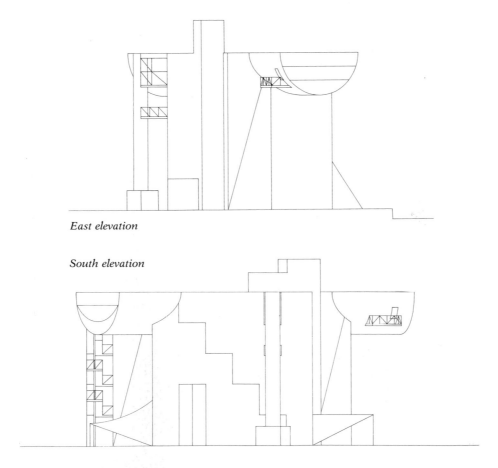

East elevation

South elevation

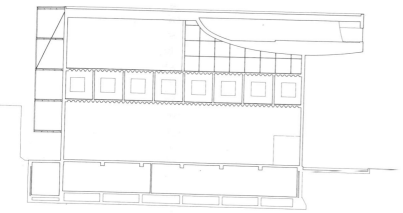

Longitudinal section

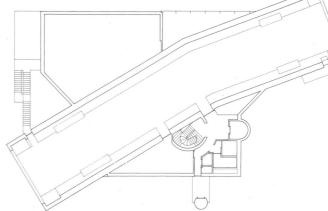

Fourth floor plan

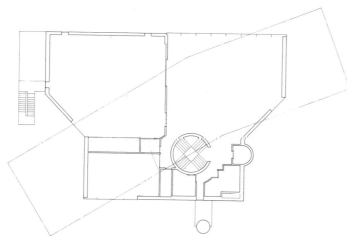

Third floor plan

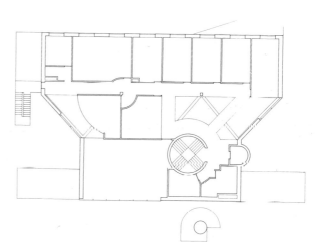

Second floor plan

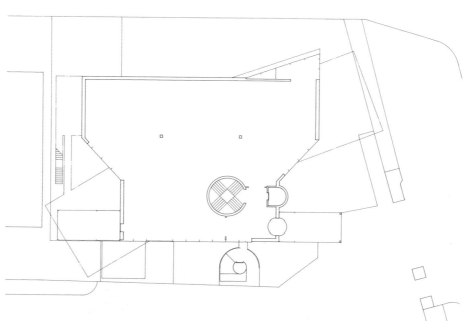

First floor plan

HIROSHI HARA

Yamato International • Tokyo • 1987

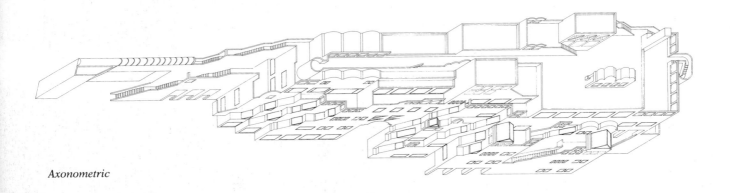

Axonometric

Situated in a warehouse district, this headquarter building for Yamato International, a Japanese fashion fabric enterprise, in fact stands on reclaimed land along Tokyo Bay. Although this relatively new land in Tokyo is rapidly attracting construction, the park extending in front will keep the sight of its façade undisturbed. The three lower floors of delivery rooms and storage form what might be called a platform, upon which stands the structure of the upper five stories of offices.

The following points were the main ideas in designing the building:

City within architecture:

Transverse section

the façade composed of twelve vertical strata is intended to appear as the epitome of urban scenery.

The exterior, covered with aluminum panels, is the reflector of its surrounding climate; its sensitively shifting appearance corresponds to the changing nature of the environment. Thus, contrary to an immutable edifice, it represents perpetual change or *mujo*, the traditional Japanese aesthetic concept of transience or ephemerality.

Unlike most modern office buildings that are dominated by homogeneous and uniform space, this building is planned so that

every place in its interior is different from the others. This is carried to such an extent that no two etching patterns on window panes are identical.

Image, reflection and overlay evoked by stone walls and glass windows transiently change the atmosphere in the interiors and on the terraces. Because of such uncertain boundaries, every interior space is rendered undefinable.

Numerous kinds of paths are devised inside and out of this building via the bridge and terraces, which stem from the main route of the sky circuit that leads through the courtyard, the ascending staircase, across the bridge, the roof-deck, several stairways, the terrace on the fourth floor, and then back to the courtyard. *H. Hara*

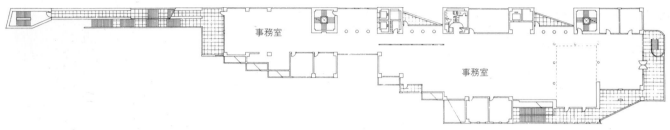

Sixth floor plan

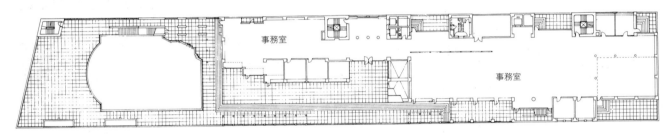

Fourth floor plan

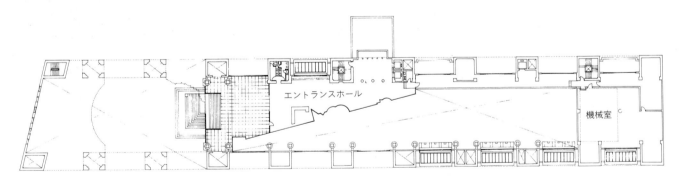

Second floor plan

Axonometric, detail

Iida City Museum • 1988

This building is a municipal cultural complex. It consists of an art museum, a museum of regional natural history, a multipurpose gallery, an auditorium, and a planetarium. The art museum mainly exhibits the painting collection of Shunso Nishida, who was born in this city and is one of the Japanese artists represented.

Kunio Yanagida, the founder of Japanese folklore studies, was also born in Iida. His old house and that of another locally-born poet were moved and reconstructed on this site. Together with several of the castle's restored ruins (moat, wells, and water conduits), the whole site and adjoining old shrine are designed as a museum park containing historical and local relics.

The roof terrace of this building, planned to become part of this park, can be approached without entering the building.

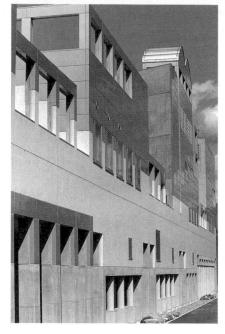

There, one can view the Akaishi Mountains, commonly called the Southern Alps, which lie to the east. Iida is situated in the valley between this mountain range and another 3,000-meter range, the Central Alps. The sight of the Southern Alps is ingrained in the people here. Its silhouette inspired the design of the roof over the eighty-meter-long main lobby. This roof, supported by tree-like concrete columns and steel trusses, was designed to evoke images of a forest, like those around the shrine, in the nearby mountains, or in our memories.

The exhibition spaces required a controllable environment devoid of natural light necessary for the preservation of delicate old Japanese paintings. The resulting uniformity and homogeneity of these spaces form the platform for the roof terrace and the main lobby which, on the contrary, are non-uniform, transient spaces; they change with the season, time, and climate. *H. Hara*

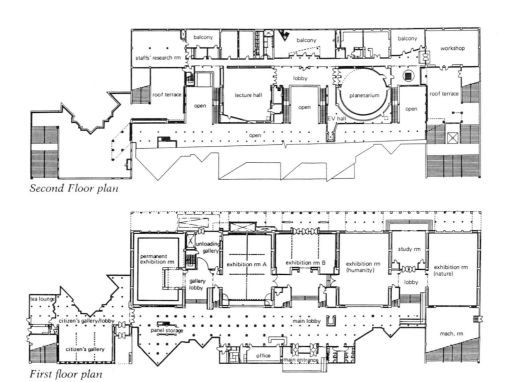

Second Floor plan

First floor plan

HIROMI FUJII

*Ushimado International Arts Festival Center • Okayama
Prefecture • 1985*

This project began with an old storehouse that was left from the Edo period and stood on the site. Architects generally respond to such a condition with fusion or contrast, harmonizing the design with the environment in question or relating the two in some other way. I disregarded such conventional methods, however, and began by metamorphosing the old, existing storehouse. This is not the first time I have used the method I call metamorphology, wherein transformation of formal and spatial codes of architecture, if repeated, cause forms and spaces to lose their coding and eventually to become traces of their originals. The meaning that the forms and spaces possessed before their transformation is neither retained nor entirely eliminated in the traces; these traces exist in an intermediate domain that is neither one nor the other.

More interesting are questions of what it is we feel when we encounter this building and what the traces generate upon that encounter. The fragmentary differentiation induced by the traces may suggest...what?... historic ruins? It may in fact suggest something else. The metamorphosing of the old storehouse involved first of all identifying and then rearranging the characteristics of the storehouse. Openings and solid walls of exposed concrete, for example, are set in opposition to geometric walls with gridded joints, to disconnected, fragmentary surfaces, and to walls that define interior and exterior spaces. The architectural elements of the lounge building are all reversals of the elements of the office building; openings and solid walls in the office building become respectively solid walls and openings in the lounge building. The repeated metamorphoses eventually produce a balcony space. Yet, as a result of these transformations,

we no longer can say with cer-
tainty or exactitude what this
space is. If our world is built up
through the accretion of everyday
experience and thereby becomes
meaningful, then this can be said
to be a deconstructed space that
has escaped the confines of our
world. *H. Fujii*

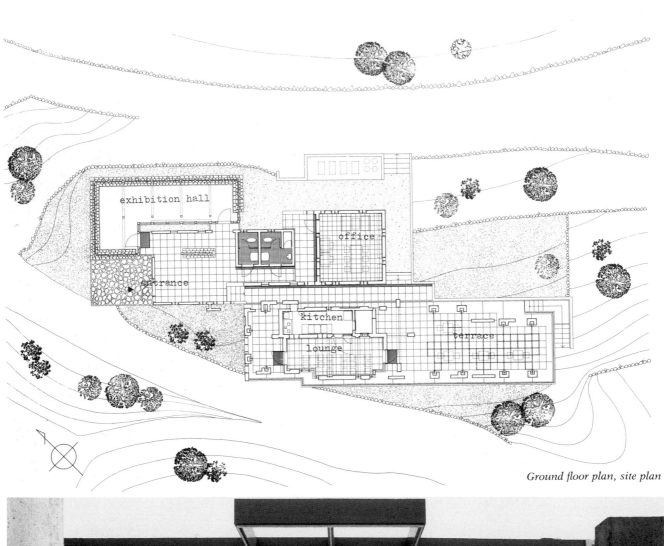

Ground floor plan, site plan

Project Mizoe No. 1 · Iizuka City · 1988

For several years now—as I designed the Ushimado International Arts Festival Center, the Second Gymnasium at the Shibaura Institute of Technology, and the Project Mizoe No. 1 presented here—I have been trying to organize my thoughts concerning both a multi-layered quality of space and the "inscription" of that quality. I initially developed the idea of a multilayered quality of space in response to a desire to escape from, or reject, the compositional principles that govern the creation of classical architecture—namely balance, harmony, stability, and unity.

In contemplating both the world of classicism and reality with all its variety and complexity, I am forced to consider the diverse visions that the latter affords. In considering the diverse world of reality, we must first realize that we are a part of it. The same can be said of our everyday language. The viewing subject, which we once regarded as a mirror reflecting immutable images, possesses distortions like language and is a part of that world as well. That being the case, a stable and closed construct cannot possibly serve as a model of diversity.

A model that will serve this purpose is one in which our vision is a diverse and complex mosaic which, by continuously shifting in a world akin to a series of boxes within boxes, perceives the traces of that world and manages, to a limited extent, to crystallize and systematize them. This process is what I earlier referred to as inscription, and I take a multi-layered space to be a space with a structure that generates such a vision.

The space in the Project Mizoe no. 1, which is a model house with a required flexible plan, is generated by four L-shaped walls that result from disassembling a cube. These walls are covered by a 1.8 meter by 1.8 meter grid, and half that size of 0.9 meter by 0.9 meter is used to indicate the backs of walls. Walls other than these four have been carved by a 0.6 meter by 0.6 meter grid to show that they have a different character and role. As one threads one's way past these walls into the entrance and then into the house, the grids become layered and one's vision continually shifts. The light introduced by the gridded openings also changes from moment to moment and serves to alter the building's expression. *H. Fujii*

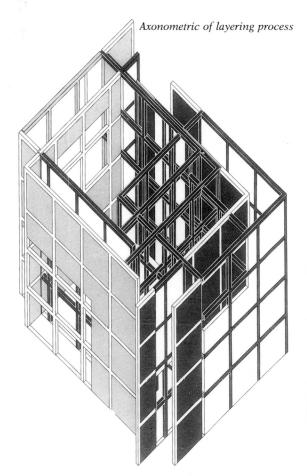

Axonometric of layering process

First floor plan

Second floor plan

N

MINORU TAKEYAMA

Tokyo International Port Terminal • 1991

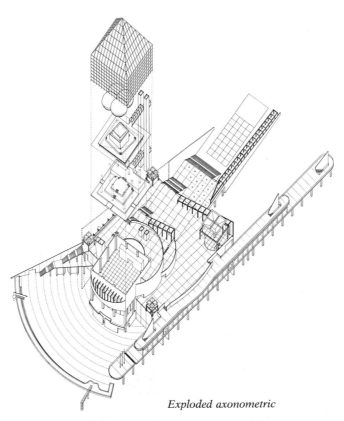

Exploded axonometric

The Terminal Building is located at the edge of reclaimed land in the harbor, along the waterfront of Tokyo Bay, and forms a symbolic gate between the water and the city. Since the extent of the reclamation remains uncertain, the new facility is planned to be a landmark for the surrounding environment.

The Terminal building is intended to convey a multiplicity of messages in a single language, signifying, among others, the land of relief that travelers first encounter after a long voyage, and, for the citizens, a point of reference indicating where the land meets with the water. In the overall syntax, two intersecting axes play dominant roles: one is parallel with the water edge; the other is visually oriented toward the remote views of the still heavily-industrialized seascape and the new suspension bridge, to be completed in 1993, which is to also serve as a gate to the whole bay.

The main facilities, immigration and customs clearance areas, offices, and waiting lobby are arranged under a platform that rises from the entrance plaza on street level up to the main roof garden, and continues down to the waterfront park to the north of the terminal. The open space at the western edge, which has the water screen (a chain of water and fog fountains), will act as a transition between the sea water and the man-made environment. The upper facilities, a hall, a restaurant, a port gallery, and an open-air observation deck, are designed as an airy composition, with solids and voids. Its house-like quality is expressed by the steel-frame pyramid, creating a single and powerful landmark for travelers, against the unstable cityscape, and for the downtowners, against the industrial vernacular that surrounds them in the port area.

The four membranous domes over the observation deck within the pyramid will be lit from inside after dark, yet with no explicit messages to convey. The Terminal is to be completed in 1991 in commemoration of the fiftieth anniversary of the appointment of the International Port of Tokyo. *M. Takeyama*

TAKEFUMI AIDA

Kazama House • Kawaguchi • 1987

The site is surrounded by a mixture of old vernacular houses, new tract houses, and farmland. The estates of the past have largely disappeared, but this site retains some of the atmosphere of an estate. On the nearly 1,000-square-meter property stand a number of zelkova trees that are over fifty years old, and along the street is a big cherry tree. The arrangement of planes in the Kazama House was largely determined by the trees and the street to the south of the property.

In order to provide unobstructed views of the trees, which are concentrated primarily on the east side of the site, the planes are oriented east-west (i.e., parallel to the X-axis). These spaces, each sandwiched between a pair of walls, create an exaggerated sense of perspective and emphasize the transparency in the direction of the trees in the garden. Windows on the south side were kept to a minimum. This is also intended to assure privacy from the street and to articulate a hierarchy of privacy along the north-south axis (i.e., the Y-axis). Nearest to the street is the spatial layer containing the guest room and living room. Separated from it by a corridor is the next layer containing the kitchen, courtyard, and main bedroom. Beyond another corridor is the layer containing the bathroom and toilet. Between layers, I introduced aluminum *shoji* covered with perforated aluminum panels to let interior and exterior spaces flow together.

I also added house-shaped walls 50 millimeters from the exterior walls in order to create a multi-layered composition. The *shoji* screens are not slid into walls, but they are slid behind the walls of the *tatami* rooms. Windows were created without relationship to the *shoji* screens. The two systems are independent, though contiguous. The exterior walls in the X-axis direction are

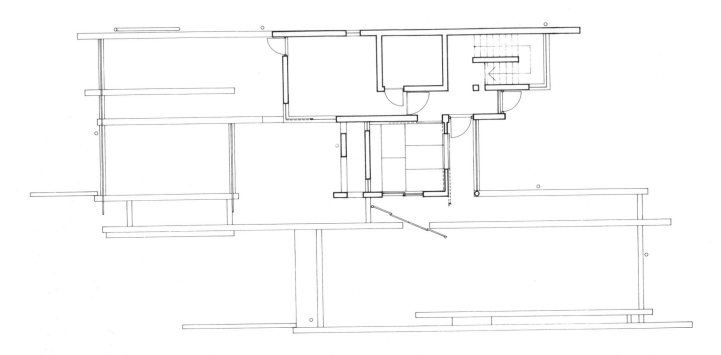

Second floor plan

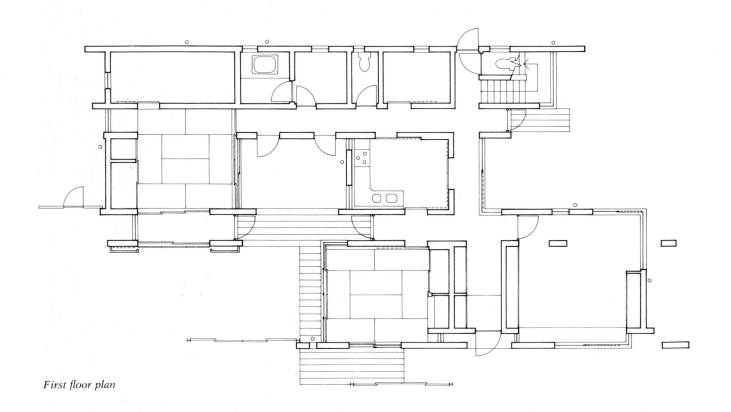

First floor plan

colored light grey, and those in the Y-axis direction have been made white. Making the difference in value very slight and creating openings have made glimpses of trees and the sky possible and have rendered the impression of the building ambiguous. In this way, I have sought to amplify the concept of fluctuation. *T. Aida*

TADAO ANDO
Time's I & II • Kyoto • 1985 • 1991

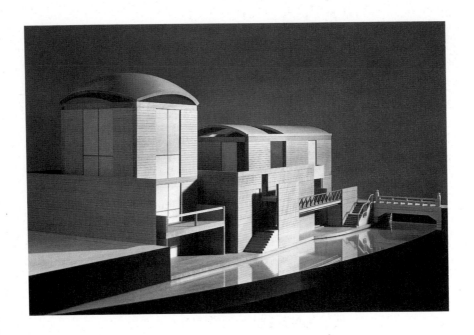

The site is at the foot of the bridge called Sanjo Kobashi which spans the Takase River in Kyoto. The height of the buildings here is restricted to three floors, thus the volumes of both the first and second phase have been arranged not to strike out into the middle of the city. Their blending with the environment is also assured by the limited range of modest materials: concrete block, rough-textured black granite, and steel. The intention was to use concrete block in a new way, treating it carefully and not as a rough material. Time's I, the first phase, is covered by a vaulted roof, oriented parallel to the river and cut at the end to reveal its section.

An outer wall, following the property line on the west side, keeps the crowd of adjacent structures at bay. On the other side, however, the street is drawn into the heart of the building while the building relates to the river in various ways, creating a complexity of spaces. The first floor is nearly at water level, where a small plaza is designed in the shape of a sixth of a circle. The stairway descending to this plaza gives the observer a foretaste of the interplay between the river and the building. Each store is approached not from the street side, but from the direction of the

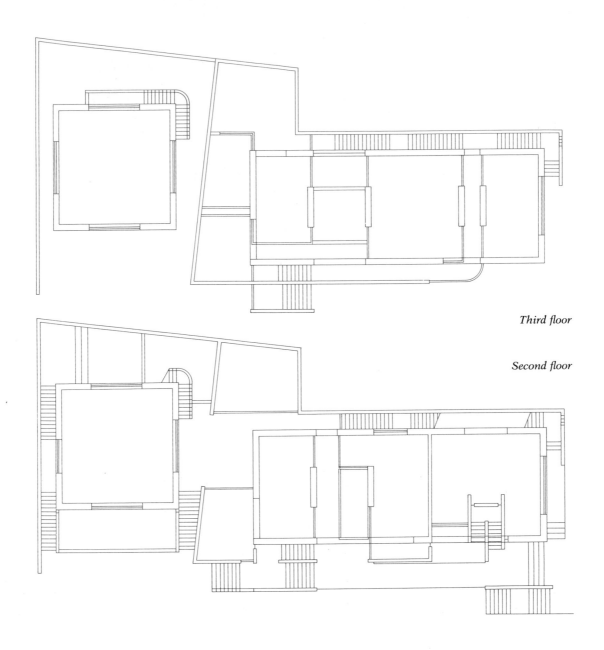

Third floor

Second floor

river. As a result, the stores are linked to the river, and from each of them a different view of the river is revealed.

At the second level, which is continuous with the street, a passageway wraps around the building and enters through a deck.

This arrangement endows the simple geometry of the building with a maze-like complexity. In walking between the spatially distinct stores, one can suddenly come upon either the view of the sky or varyingly angled views of the river. Places open to the river

and places open to the sky are scattered throughout the building; these are joined and create a rich overall composition.

If, in the first phase, the theme was the relationship of people to the river as I attempted to draw the landscape into the

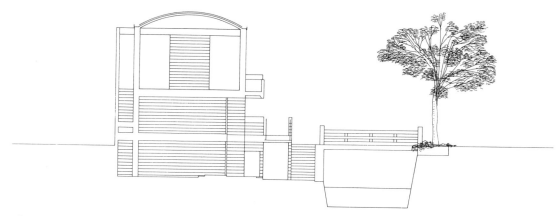

Elevation, transverse river section

Elevation, transverse street section

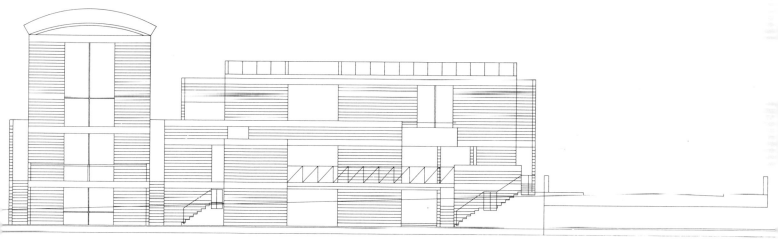

building, in Time's II the objective is to extend the plaza along the river. The building is composed of a three-story volume with an eight-meter square plan; a wall around this volume follows the property line. The roof's form is a dome, as opposed to the vault of the first phase. While the vault expressed the axis of the river flow, the dome emphasizes the building's centrality. The passageway, which comes in from the street, is wrapped around the building and comes to a stop, but the plaza continues at a different level. With this addition, when completed, the circulation quality of the spaces in the composition is greatly increased. *T. Ando*

TADAO ANDO   117

Galleria Akka • Osaka   • *1988*

Galleria Akka is yet another commercial project of Tadao Ando's in which, as a Calvino-esque carver of imaginary cities, he continues his determination to subvert the Japanese urban chaos by inserting into it concrete townscapes of his own making. The familiarity of the Galleria's architecture stems from the repetitious orthodoxy of his design method, which produces buildings with a predictable variation of spatial ideas. However, this predictability becomes a more intriguing aspect of Ando's architecture as one discovers that, given the large number of his works, these designs transcend their singular meanings and start to reveal an incessant intention to plant the seeds of a different city. Seen in this way, Ando's buildings appear in the Japanese urban landscape as fragments of another, parallel and potential city that has been carved into, or excavated from, the substance of the existing one.

Formally, the Galleria is derivative of Ando's particular design method in which the encasement of the site within a concrete box denotes the primary act of making architecture. This operation is devised to eliminate the city as a physical context and produce an abstract void—the site—as a fixed place and a predictable context for the building into which meaning can be projected and reciprocated. It signifies an almost ritualistic attitude toward the idea of (re)creating the city. By establishing a territory for his own city, the design process for Ando becomes an almost autonomous operation concentrated on the generation of a specific urban condition within

Section

the building itself. This condition—the texture of Ando's imaginary city—is actualized through the dialectic opposition between solids and voids which are kept in equilibrium by means of parti walls within the concrete enclosure. Consequently, these walls act as double instruments for the articulation of building form and the carving of urban space.

The curved wall in Galleria Akka is both a texture and a matrix: it is the tangible substance of a city and the vessel of its myths, revealing itself to the dweller as a path between the primordial darkness of the city foundations and the ethereal light of the sky above it. The corporeal presence of the wall stands in antithetical opposition to the

ephemera of the outside city, replacing it with the concreteness of a phenomenal world. At the same time the wall is a segment of a circle that, along the extension of its imaginary circumference, points beyond itself, implying the notion of a larger whole, which exceeds the confinement of the concrete box and traces the matrix of a different city. Traces of an "other" city perpetually reoccur in the fragmentary elements of the building's form. The top floor bridge, for instance, halted and suspended in mid-air, projects into the void, evoking the existence of an unknown urban territory to which its missing end belongs. The incompleteness of the bridge signifies the untenability of this territory existing in the realm of Ando's poetic imagination. The fragmentary character of formal elements creates not only dramatic interstitial spaces and a sense of dynamism but, by eliminating the centrality of space, also disrupts the self-enclosed system of architectural signification. Hence, the concrete box of the building does not appear as a self-contained piece of architecture but rather as an excavated part of Ando's imaginary city where immediate relationships between the constituting spatial and formal elements, through the fragmented nature of their form, suggest the existence of a larger urban structure of which they are parts. Consequently, the Galleria Akka can be best understood as a sequel to Ando's narration about an imaginary city whose new parts are being revealed and told through the voids carved within the building's concrete enclosure.
Vladimir Krstic

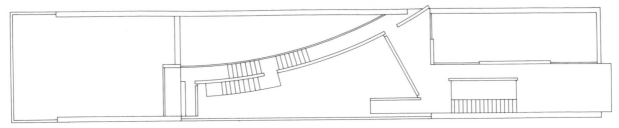

Fourth floor

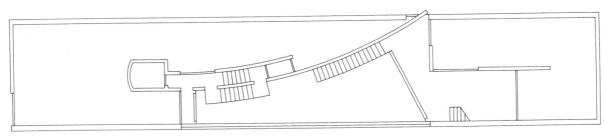

Third floor

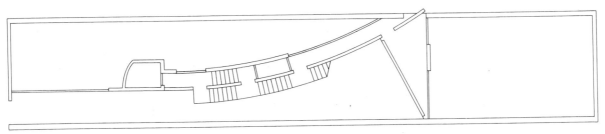

Second floor

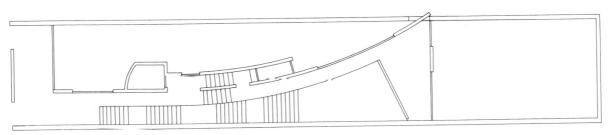

First floor

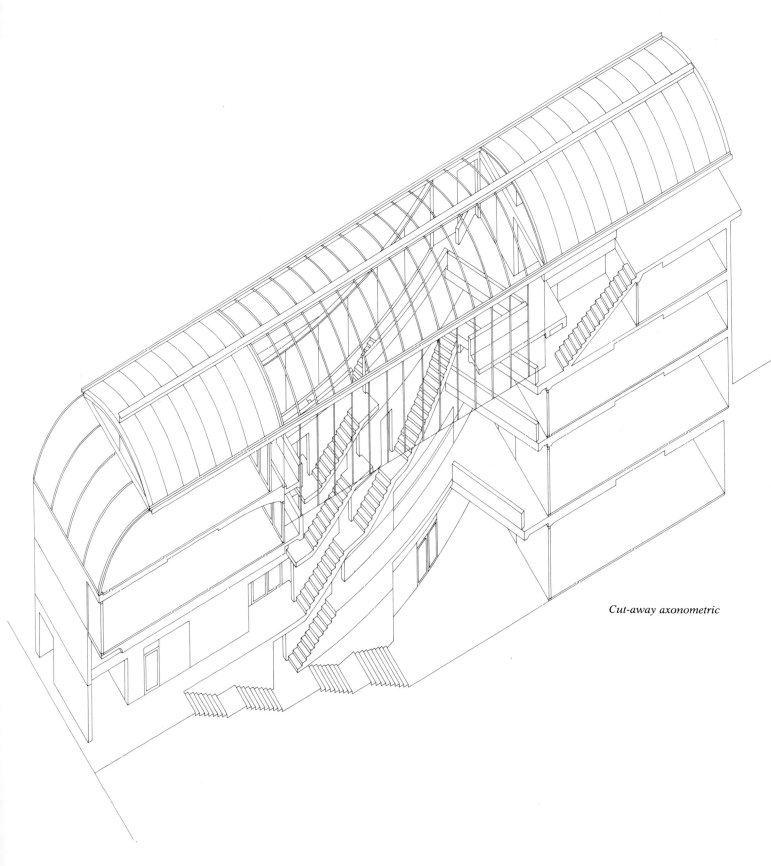

Cut-away axonometric

Church with Light · Ibaraki · Osaka Prefecture · 1989

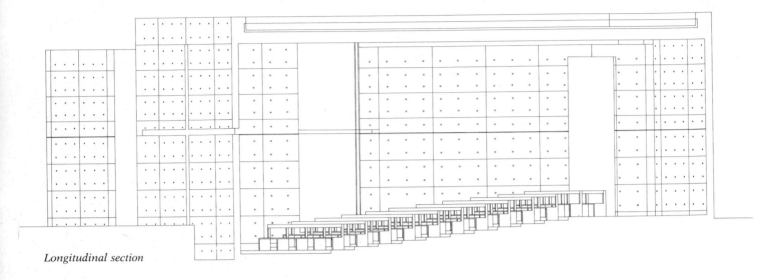

Longitudinal section

Contemporary architecture is under the sway of economic rationalism. Everything is determined by cost, and there is no room for human consideration. Is it impossible for architecture to exist today other than as a commercial product? Things are treated as consumer goods; they are manufactured and disappear. It is as if the human act of making or using were something to be despised or ashamed of. This work raises questions about the present condition. It is significant in that it reaffirmed for me the notion that the economically rational is not the only way in which things can be made.

This church is located in a quiet residential district in Ibaraki City, Osaka Prefecture. A chapel and the minister's house, both of wood construction, existed on the site, and the church was planned as an addition; it was sited on the basis of its relationship to the earlier buildings and its solar orientation. It is a cube in which three spheres, each with a diameter of 5.9 meters, could be inscribed; its interior is penetrated by a wall angled at 15°. This diagonal wall is 18 centimeters lower than the building proper and divides the space into a chapel and an entrance area. From the entrance, one passes through an opening made in the diagonal wall, and turns 180° to arrive at the church. The floor descends in stages toward the altar. A cruciform has been cut out of the wall behind the altar, and the morning sun entering through it creates a cross of light.

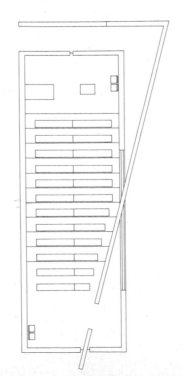

Recent works of architecture seem to lack a tactile dimension. Here, the floor and the seats have been made of rough planks used for scaffolding. This has lowered the cost and produced a more definite feeling of material. I have always used natural materials in those parts of a building that come into contact with the human hand or foot because I am convinced that substances such as wood and concrete are invaluable materials for architecture and that one becomes aware of the true quality of architecture through the body.

I made as few openings as possible in the building, because the light becomes brilliant only against a very dark background. The only natural element here is the sunlight, which is introduced to the interior in a way which renders nature extremely abstract. The architecture, adapting to this light, becomes purified. The light forms a pattern on the floor. In the shifting cross of light, one may come to recognize, in a fundamental way, the relationship of humanity to nature. *T. Ando*

KUNIHIKO HAYAKAWA

Three Houses in Seijo • Tokyo • 1982 • 1983 • 1988

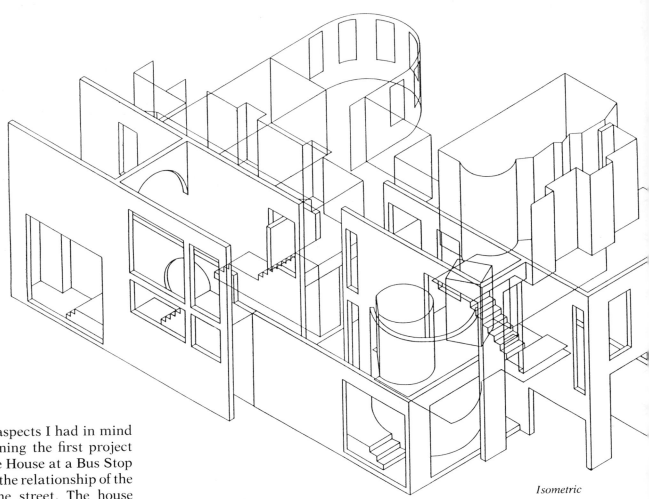

Isometric

One of the aspects I had in mind when designing the first project in Seijo, the House at a Bus Stop (1982), was the relationship of the house to the street. The house faced a disproportionately wide street, and in addition, was in front of a bus stop. These conditions prompted me to design the house with multiple layers of walls with openings facing the street. These walls, by way of the in-between domain, generate a clear spatial gradation, and filter out much of the disturbing and unwanted effects created by the busy road in front. In other words, the walls make communication between the inside and

outside more indirect. On the other hand, through the carefully arranged openings, the house is able to transmit to the street a proper degree of signs of life within.

In the case of the second project, the House at a Crossroad (1983), the living quarters and studio of a pianist, joined by an entrance, are arranged in an L

around a fifty-year-old tulip tree that is over 20 meters high. Like the House at a Bus Stop, this house is centered around an interior "landscape," a vaulted space called the gallery. Openings are reduced to the bare minimum to reduce noise from the street. By lowering the floor of the living room below ground level, the gasoline stand directly to the south has been rendered invisible from inside the house. Although the site is relatively large, the building is not actively related to its context; instead, connections with its surroundings had to be cut off, a fate that is common to houses in Japanese cities. These houses turn their back on the environment and take an inward-oriented, defensive position. As a consequence, the street is defined by the backs of houses. The House at a Crossroads and House at a Bus Stop were planned as stage-sets in order to give them a closed-yet-open expression that enabled them to relate to the unfriendly environment in a cautious manner, through multiple layers of walls with limited openings.

The third project, the House Between, was constructed between the two earlier ones. In the previous cases, I had to consider and design the houses not only from the occupants' point of view, but also from the pedestrians'. This approach was taken also in the design of the House Between. With the addition of Between, more than 30 meters of multi-layered walls face the street, establishing and modulating an open-yet-closed relationship between the private and public domains of the city. *K. Hayakawa*

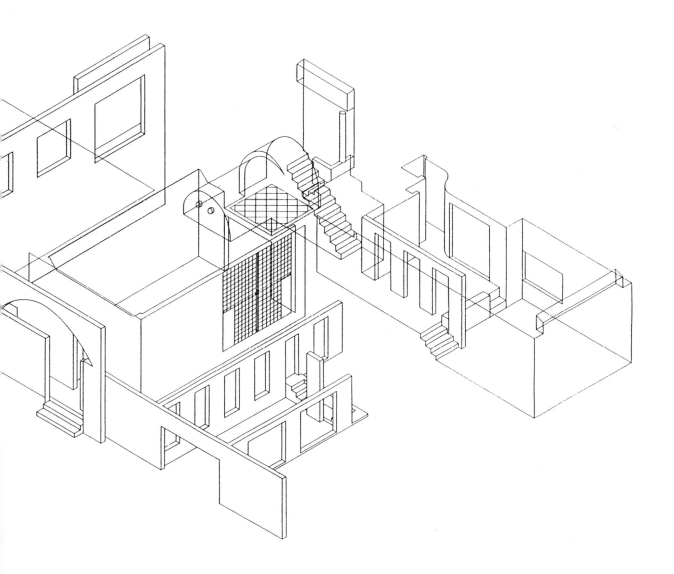

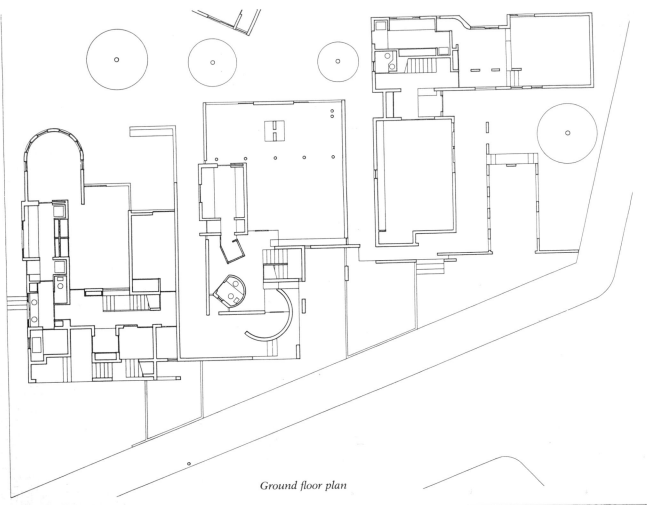

Ground floor plan

TOYO ITO

Silver Hut • Tokyo • 1984

My own house is comprised of independent concrete columns on a 3.6-meter grid with seven vaulted roofs curving gently between them. The largest vault, with a span twice as long as the others, covers the central courtyard and is covered with a manually operated tent structure for revealing the sky. The other six vaults which surround this central vault cover the living room, dining room, kitchen, bedrooms, and Japanese room. The ranks of these vaulted roofs appear as a cluster of small primitive huts.

The entire house is one story except the bedrooms, which are made into two levels by slightly lowering the ground floor level. Furthermore, almost the entire floor area, including the central courtyard, is covered with traditional Japanese roof tiles, which evokes a memory of the classic compact earth floor that was typical in *minka*, the Japanese folk house.

In addition, and in contrast to, the classic roof tiles, contemporary materials are also used in abundance. The roofs and walls, both interior and exterior, are made of aluminum sheets, zinc alloy sheets, and other metallic materials. Most of the furniture is also made of metallic materials and is designed in such a way that

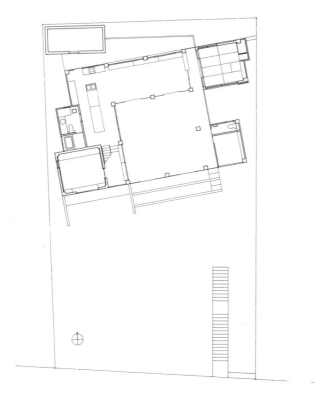

Plan

Orthographic

the height can be freely adjusted by means of air dampers. The twenty-three skylights and bull's-eye windows are equipped with automobile parts and present an overall image of a spaceship making a landing.

These two distinctively different sets of images—one of a primitive hut such as a traditional *minka*-style house, and the other of a spaceship of highly advanced technology—may appear at first sight to contradict each other. However, it is precisely this juxtaposition that the city of Tokyo exhibits today. A primitive hut designed for dwelling in a modern, urban environment, just as ancient people made their primitive huts with logs, would be a silver-colored hut as is this house, and made of metallic materials which are easily available today.

As the basic structure of this house consists of concrete columns and steel frames, no walls bear any structural load. Therefore, without any lateral restric-tions, the structure provides quite open-ended spaces, as in the traditional wooden houses of Japan. This open-endedness of the space is further enriched with the qualities of lightness, suppleness, and transparency by using sheer perforated aluminum screens, white paper *washi* screens called *shoji*, and fabric tents, which give the appearance of gently covering the whole space with a thin membrane. *T. Ito*

Pastina Restaurant · Tokyo · 1989

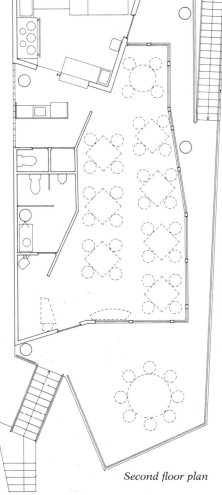

Second floor plan

This building is a small-scale commercial complex that includes a restaurant. It faces a busy street in one of the suburbs of Tokyo. A space of three floors, two stories above and one underground, has been created under an airy roof that reminds one of a flapping tent sheet. This roof is built by combining, in alternate fashion, thin, triangular boards of 5-meter base length with steel-frame construction, the boards forming the ridge line. The lower two floors have a reinforced concrete Rahmen structure, and the roof board is partly mounted on the six independent pillars, partly suspended by steel pillars extending from the reinforced concrete pillars. Beneath the roof, a restaurant enveloped in aluminum sashes and tent sheets, is connected to a wooden terrace that resembles the deck of a ship. The lower two floors are for rent, and amenities are secured by a light court dug to the maximum extent on the western side of the site. Walls surrounding each space on the stories above ground are constructed by inserting different materials for each span according to function. *T. Ito*

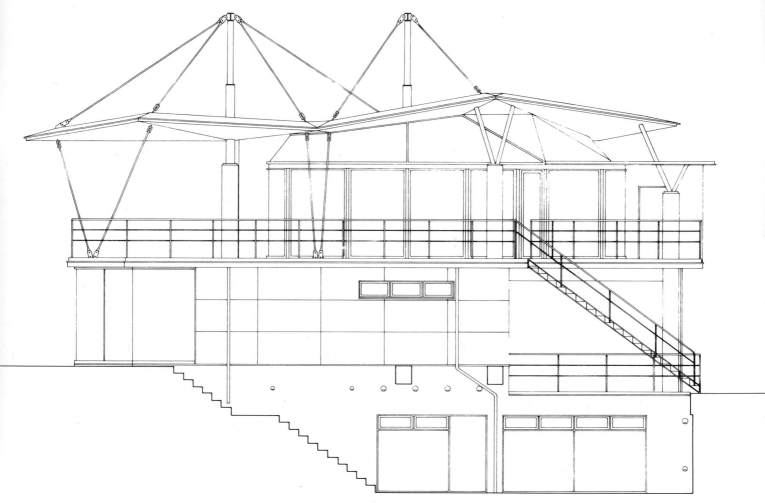

Side elevation

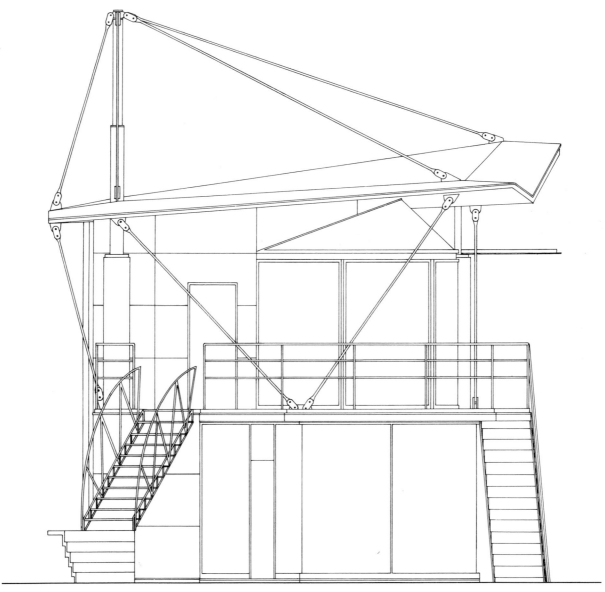

Street elevation

ITSUKO HASEGAWA

House in Oyamadai • Tokyo • 1988.

Each time one designs a house, one makes a statement not merely about architectural forms or materials, but about life. One communicates ideas about countless actions and objects. When I reflect upon the houses I have designed, I feel that I have continually tried to create works that were "unfinished," in touch with reality, and related to the times.

Just prior to this House in Oyamadai, I designed a house in Higashi—Tamagawa, Tokyo. There, my aim was to make it possible for the occupants to enjoy a comfortable urban life while remaining in contact with na-

ture. In the center of that house was a circular courtyard, and on the second floor, a terrace.

The House in Oyamadai is a sequel to that design. In contrast to the courtyard in Higashi Tamagawa, which is completely enclosed and open only to the sky, this courtyard is smaller (4.5 meter in diameter), open to the street and integrated with the city. It provides light in the manner of a small garden in a traditional townhouse. The boundary between inside and outside is more ambiguous. The space visible from the courtyard is articulated by many linear elements and has a character that is in

sympathy with the Tokyo landscape.

One approaches the house by way of a lightweight steel stairway, at the top of which there is an outdoor room in front of the entrance. From there, one can see the surrounding landscape framed by semi-transparent screens and slender framing members. The second floor is one room, arranged in a circular fashion, which accommodates the reception, dining, kitchen, and living areas. The south side consists entirely of windows of perforated metal screen on the outside, sash on the inside, and translucent acrylic *shoji*-like

First floor plan

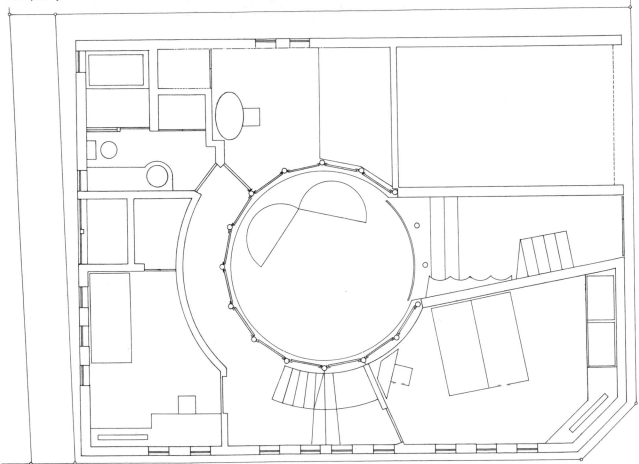

Second floor plan

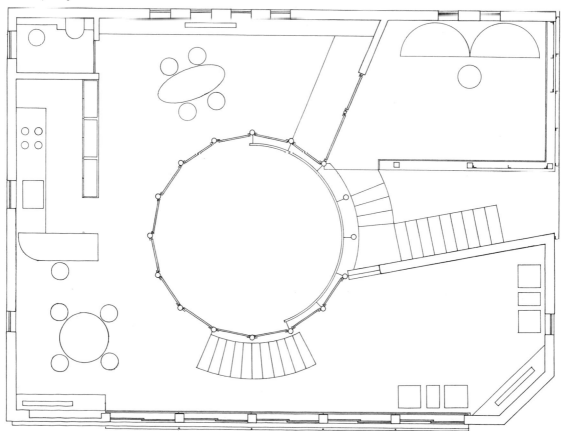

screens in between. Together, these elements create a bright wall. Thanks to the circular courtyard and the wall, the entire second floor is well lit and well ventilated. The bedrooms were situated on the first floor to assure privacy. A game room and a ga-

rage, accessible by a ramp, are in the basement.

In urban areas around the world, and in Tokyo in particular, architecture has become hard and closed, taking on less and less significance. People are becoming alert to this condition and de-

siring more open and sensitive design that responds both to increasing density and their changing lifestyles. Architecture can become open only when it takes human behavior into account. *I. Hasegawa*

Shonandai Cultural Center • Fujisawa City • 1989 (First phase)

South elevation

The Shonandai Cultural Center is based on a proposal that won an open competition held by Fujisawa City. The fact that it was a combination of children's pavilion, community center, and public theater attracted me the most to the project. In explaining my entry to the competition, I wrote that "in order to achieve its public objectives, the building must be a place that can bring together and adapt to many different classes of people: children and the elderly, women and men, the handicapped and those without handicaps. This should be

thought of not as a single building, but as a complex, one that provides a special place. This special place should have many different faces and be in constant flux; it should be able to accommodate multiple events and contain within it not only the world but the universe."

Right after I was formally commissioned to design the center, I was given the opportunity, much to my surprise, to have direct contact with the citizens of Fujisawa. This was because many residents objected to the creation of an underground building. The

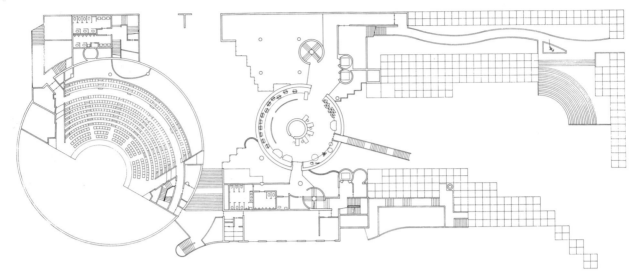

Second floor plan

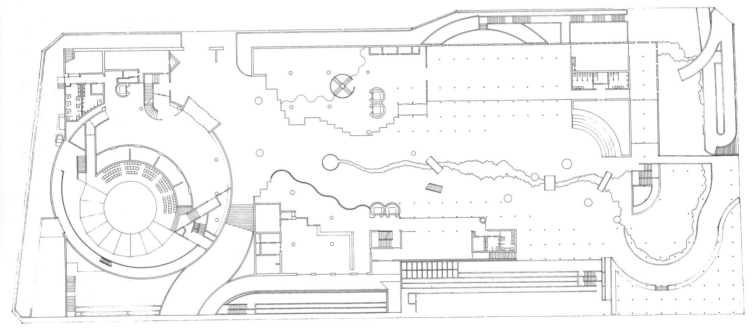

First floor plan

first exchange of views led to dozens of meetings until the completion of design. The competition entry, which expressed a strong concept, was made less assertive; it took on a group image and was transformed into a stage set for the community. The total volume of the facility is large for the site area. I fit about two-thirds of this into a modernistic box-like struc-ture that would allow freedom of planning, and buried it underground. In keeping with the theme of the center, which is to promote both roots in the local community and a better understanding of the world and the universe, spheres (a world globe, a cosmic globe, a moon globe, and a geodesic dome) that suggest a futuristic, cosmic environment, and clusters of pitched roof structures that suggest the woods or a village of folk houses, have been built above the ground. The plaza is a man-made garden characterized by a stream, a pond, greenery, and various shelters; a path allows visitors to stroll through a roof garden. One can walk past a cluster of roofs suggesting a mountain of rocks, the earth and

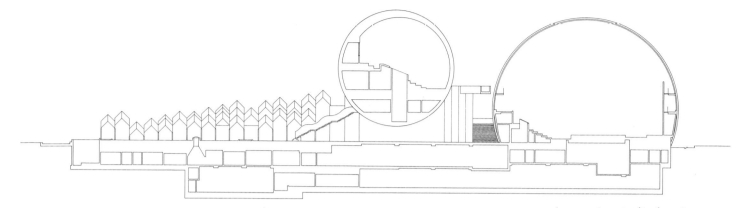

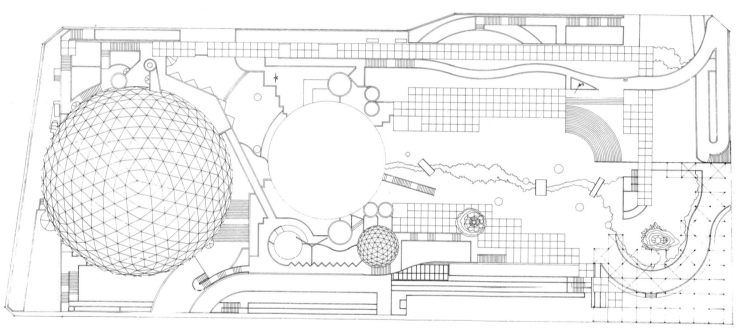

cosmic globes. Devices that are activated by light, wind and sound, a tower of wind and light, and a "tree" with a built-in clock have been installed along the way. The below-ground rooms and corridors face a sunken garden where one feels embraced by nature.

For several years my practice has been based on the con-cept of architecture as another form of nature. Instead of think-ing of architecture as something to be constructed according to reason and differentiated from other forms of matter, architec-ture, I feel, should be inscribed and legible in terms of the aspects of nature. A basic theme of this project was to accept those things that had been rejected by the spirit of rationalism—the trans-lucent world of emotions and the supple and comfortable space woven by nature—and to create a landscape filled with a new form of nature where devices en-able one to hear the strange mu-sic of the universe. *I. Hasegawa*

ITSUKO HASEGAWA   157

KAZUNARI SAKAMOTO

House F • Tokyo • 1988

Within the context of a city where highways plunge through residential mazes, Eastern and Western ideologies coexist without blending, nostalgia vies with tomorrow's fashion and egotistical expression struggles under a cloak of national anonymity, Kazunari Sakamoto is searching for a house appropriate for modern Tokyo. His aim is to create an environment that nurtures living, rather than an object toting familiar façades that evoke outmoded notions of a house.

In House F Sakamoto has erected an Asian idea of shelter in the undulating roof supported by branched columns. The space un-der the roof is not isolated by the structure, but remains contiguous with a universal field, which flows past the domestic realm. He uses separate architectural elements, such as the roof, column, and wall, not as a defensive order imposed upon nature, but as a method of focusing attention on specific spots within an unaffected chaos. For instance, the roof concavities resemble parabolic curves in their redirection of reflected rays onto one spot. These places become points of orientation for human action and interaction.

Yet, behind the solid, bearing walls of a Western derivation,

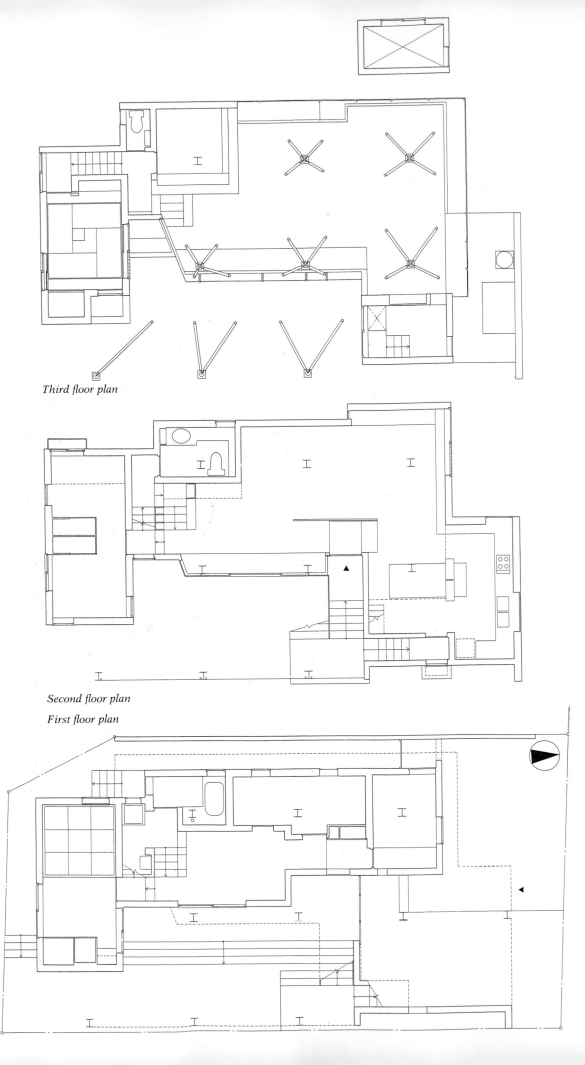

Third floor plan

Second floor plan

First floor plan

Sakamoto also provides a retreat for individual family members. Just as the family is no longer an irreducible organ set against society, the house is no longer the smallest unit of the built environment. It is fractured in order to both protect and enhance a lifestyle that cannot shut out the intrusions of a communicative society.

In House F Sakamoto honestly uses a modern vocabulary to instill human value. This represents an optimistic view of the role of architecture, one that assumes that design can influence behavior rather than be just its by-product. *Glynis M. Berry*

YASUMITSU MATSUNAGA

Inscription House • Tsukuba • 1987

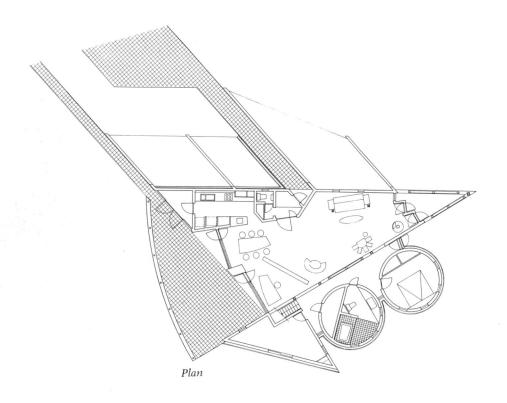

Plan

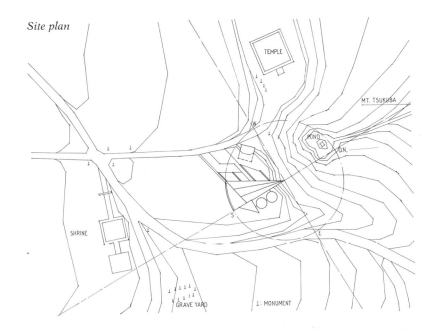

Site plan

Several years ago, when post-modern architecture still seemed to be prevailing in the world, I felt that modern civilization itself had reached the dead end of nihilism. Excessive application of historical motives, paranoiac meticulousness of high-tech expression, deliberately abstruse deconstruction, or seemingly persuasive contextualism—all these, expediously, lost their glow in my eyes while I was wandering around the world in search of the ultimately immaculate imagery that German film director Werner Herzog said would be found by a visitor from another star when he saw the green forests or

rye fields of earth. I wanted to recover unstained eyes that would see the world as it is, and I wanted to recreate architecture without any preconception, as would an angel who descended to earth for the first time. The primitive hut illustrated by Abbé Laugier was merely an example. There should be a number of images, as there are quite a variety of bird nests. The site of this house, for a computer artist in Tsukuba, is on a hill at the northeastern edge of the city, facing Mount Tsukuba right across the Sakura River. Nearby is a temple with nearly a thousand-year history. In the precinct is a dried-up pond with an island in the center. To the south is an old graveyard.

The site itself used to be a thick grove of bamboo trees full of spirits. How can we make computer art compromise with this *genius loci*?

The site was generous enough for me to conceive of a kind of earth-work that constantly emits messages of which neither the sender nor the subject will ever be revealed, like that of Nazka. So I named it Inscription, borrowing the term from Richard Serra.

On a moonlit night, a huge bird flies northward, heading for the crest of Mount Tsukuba. This giant bird has already conceived two eggs. It is impossible to tell why, although I could answer various functional questions. Be-

cause it is the most economical, the walls are finished with sheet metal, and because of passive solar considerations, the floor is finished with black mosaic tile and a ceiling fan was installed. The northwestern bank is a measure against the inclement winter storms blowing down from Mount Tsukuba. Nevertheless, these descriptions never tell anything. I only wanted to fly a giant bird. It might be because of a wish to share a portion, if only a small one, of Steiner's experience in Herzog's movie about the solitude and ecstasy of jumping, that I have been longing to fly architecture in the sky. *Y. Matsunaga*

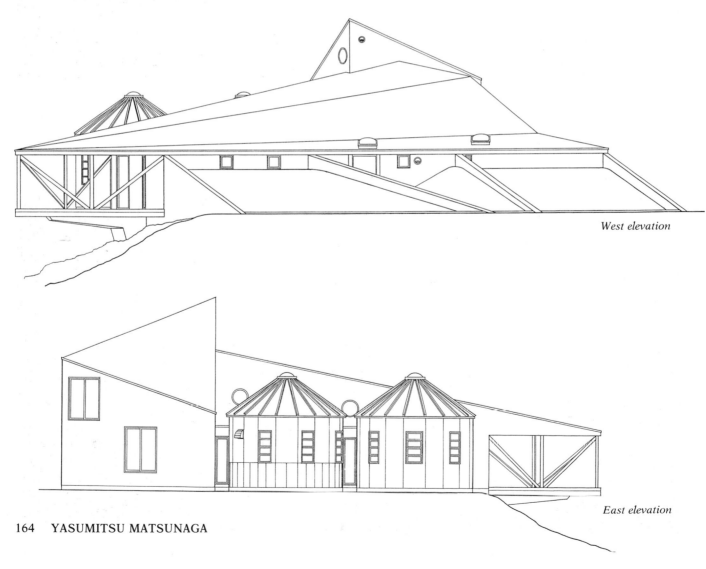

West elevation

East elevation

T-House · Higashi-Kurume · Tokyo · 1988

This is a house built for my sister in the garden of my mother's house. It called for a space for small concerts and a lot of sunlight, and was to be accomplished with minimum interference to our mother's house. This program resulted in a triangular plan with a semicircular section containing a hall on the upper level with a clerestory. On the ground level are entrance, master bedroom, study, tatami-room, bathroom, and storage. Due to the (usual) lack of budget, the structure is wood and the materials used are the most economical and commonly used ones on the market.

Just before designing this house, I was struck with the term *biophilia*, which appeared in an essay by the British critic, Peter

Fuller. This term had been originally used by the controversial American socio-biologist, E. O. Wilson, in relation to a tendency of humans to find a great deal of affinity between their creations and the shapes and structures of living organisms.

With the tremendous advancement of science, the fundamentals of epistemology are undergoing unprecedented turmoil. Particularly, what is being discovered in the fields of elementary particle physics, cosmogony, or biogenesis has seriously affected recent metaphysics. It seems to me that the frontier of science is almost approaching the sphere of transcendental thinking. This is made possible by lending all rational logic to the computer. Therefore, what is needed now is not a logical construction and operation of truth, but rather a more profound insight into it. A fusion of physics and metaphysics can probably provide us with a good understanding of *biophilia*.

Mircea Eliade, the scholar of comparative religion, defined architecture as an act of establish-

Second floor plan

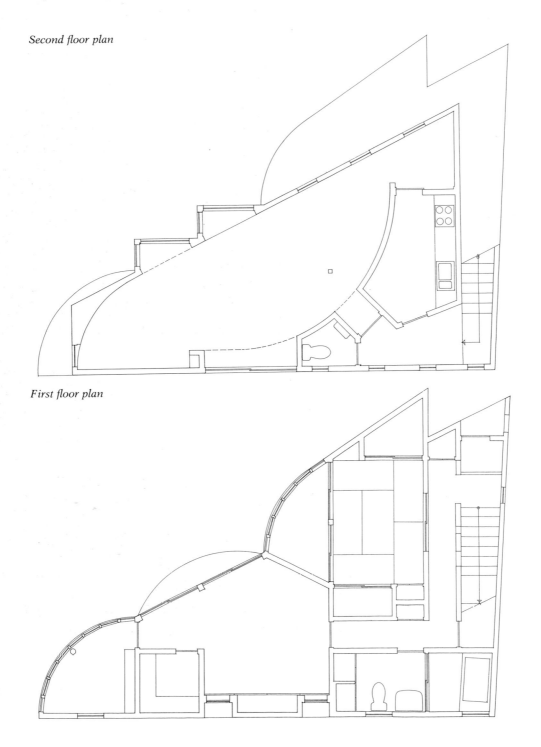

First floor plan

ing the *imago mundi*, and as such, a model of the world. If the picture of the world in the eyes of the most advanced science has been so drastically transformed, then architecture, which is supposed to reflect the world, cannot escape a serious transition either. With this recognition in mind, I started the design of this house. Although the client had been anticipating something like the conventional early-American style, she was fully satisfied with this rather peculiar solution, which somehow reminded her of a figure of a bird or a butterfly. The interior was conceived as a womb-like space filled with light, and approached through a stairway with a forced perspective. To be appropriate as an *imago mundi*, this house "contains" the sun, the moon, and stars. The entrance door has a small window glazed with a half-mirror pyramid that contains small symbols of the sun and stars; and the openings on the wall of the stairway symbolize the half-moon and stars.

The fact that this house was most heartily welcomed by the otherwise most-conservative client gave me a firm confidence in the concept of *biophilia*, as well as in the transition of the world's image that is affecting even ordinary people. I believe that we architects, who are expected to be keenly aware of the condition of human life, should never neglect this fact. *Y. Matsunaga*

OSAMU ISHIYAMA

Chohachi Art Museum • Matsuzaki–cho • 1986

There are four stages to the entire project: an art museum, an outdoor theater, a folk-craft museum, and a plaza. The first three stages have already been completed, leaving just the plaza. The last stage also involves moving a shop in front of the folk-craft museum. When that is finished, the three buildings will be linked by the plaza, which will function in part as a parking area.

The art museum houses a collection of plaster reliefs by Irie Chohachi, a plasterer renowned in his profession who was active in the late Edo and early Meiji periods. Irie was also called Izu no Chohachi and was one of the most famous craftsmen of Japan. His plaster reliefs, based on techniques to which he added his own distinctive touches, are considered works of folk art. He is considered a god in his profession, which is why a total of 2,000 plasterers, including many of the best craftsmen in Japan, gathered from all over the country to help in the construction in response to a call from the Japan Federation of Plasterers Unions. This building was designed to let them fully display their astonishing traditional plastering skills. The parts are clearly articulated, permitting the use of various techniques. Although the individual

parts of the building make use of traditional Japanese techniques, the overall form itself is not derived directly from tradition and is instead deliberately non-Japanese.

The adjacent folk-craft museum and restaurant wing, called Casa Estrellita are built with machines and are in sharp contrast. Steel, glass, and concrete are left exposed. Craftsmanly work was deliberately avoided. Here we can find two steel towers extending towards the sky, a flag of stained glass floating in the air, a gate of stars with circles, and the museum broken into pieces and reflected in the glass wall like a kaleidoscope. The two buildings were thus planned as a contrasting pair so that the character of each would be more distinct.

Nowhere in the project is the structure allowed to assert itself, and this is evident in the plans of the buildings. How to increase the independent and free-floating character of building parts is a question I intend to address in the future. *O. Ishiyama*

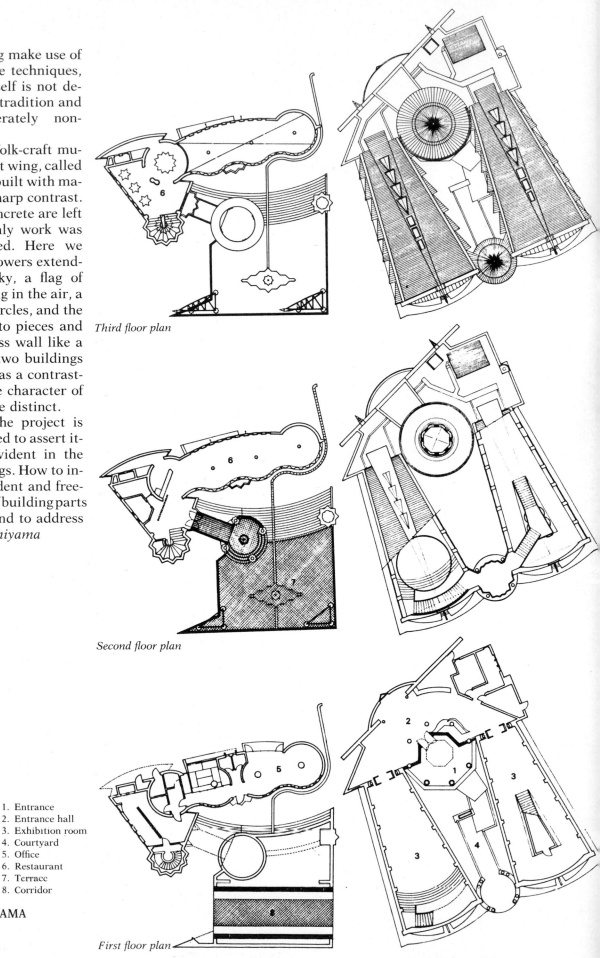

Third floor plan

Second floor plan

1. Entrance
2. Entrance hall
3. Exhibition room
4. Courtyard
5. Office
6. Restaurant
7. Terrace
8. Corridor

First floor plan

172   OSAMU ISHIYAMA

FOLK-CRAFT MUSEUM   CHOHACHI ART MUSEUM

RIKEN YAMAMOTO

Rotunda • Yokohama • 1987

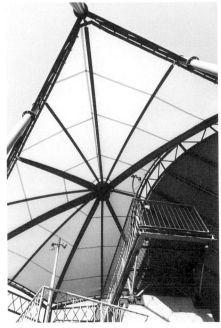

The Rotunda is a five-story, mixed-use building standing on a busy national highway in Yokohama. The first three levels are occupied by retail stores, rental offices, and rental apartments, in this order, while the fourth and fifth levels feature the owner's residence. Yamamoto's design articulates these different parts in a manner that prevents the building from appearing as an immutable or integrated whole. In fact it is as fragmented as the semi-industrial suburb that surrounds it and wherein incongruent, low-grade structures, or *zakkyo biru*, crowd the disordered landscape of the city.

Because of the juxtaposition of its contrasting elements and the extensive, though particular, use of ordinary steel products, the building acquires and ambiguous quality with regard to its context and lends itself to various interpretations. The solidly defined lower block of the building becomes an integral part of the city by filling a gap in the densely woven, but relatively low-profile urban fabric. The private residence "lands" on top of this base, and uses it as its ground or level of departure. Yamamoto refers to this understanding and intention of his by calling it the "city as topography." He explains that

Fourth floor plan

Fifth floor plan

First floor plan

Third floor plan

here "the place for *dwelling* rests on top of ... things which constitute, metaphorically speaking, the particular 'lay of the land,' that is, something like a topography. What I am trying to say is that the place for *dwelling* here rests on a topography called the city."

It is obvious then that Yamamoto's preoccupation with the Rotunda was to investigate and redefine the possibility of dwelling in, or rather over and above, the detrimental urban conditions. The city is maintained as a substratum, or perhaps archaeological site for architecture, and more so for dwelling. Over this "deposit," the eight-meter-high tubular steel columns and the covering, soft,

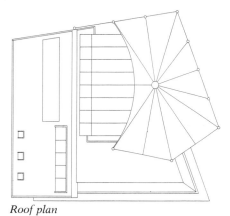
Roof plan

Teflon-fiber fabric, wrap around a spacious and airy cavity, bringing to mind archaic images and the memory of ancient tents or even cave or cliff dwellings. Within this sublime yet ambivalent realm, mediating between inside and outside worlds, as well as between the earth and the sky, are suspended various platforms and terraces, winding stairways and passages, as unique extensions of both the rituals of private dwelling and the public life of the city. The building possesses an amazing grace and a certain aloofness by which, as a place of dwelling and not unlike its archaic predecessors, it is able to keep the hostility of the environment at bay. *B. Bognar*

Hamlet • Tokyo • 1988

This project can be considered either a single, free-standing house for a large three-generation family or multi-unit housing for separate households comprised of grandparents and the families of their three children. The four households are dispersed under a huge translucent tent of Teflon, but share a terrace and a small salon, which serves as a common living room. The children's rooms are situated to be a part of their respective households yet float independently under the tent. At the same time, they appear to be gathered together, forming a chil-

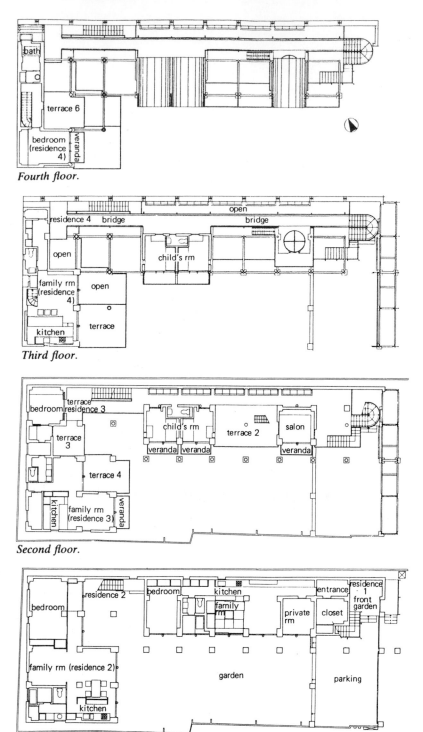

Fourth floor.

Third floor.

Second floor.

First floor; scale: 1/400.

dren's zone.

Today, dwellings are being forced out of Tokyo, where land prices are so high that only projects that promise a high return on investment can be built. Nearly everything around this residential structure has already been demolished to make way for multi-story office buildings. A house still stands next door but it, too, will eventually be replaced. The inhabitants of this new structure now live in a high-rise canyon, almost totally isolated. People should rightfully be able to live together in the city. However, in the case of Tokyo, such a position is becoming untenable. This new home is like a besieged hamlet where those who have chosen to live together in the city are making their last stand. *R. Yamamoto*

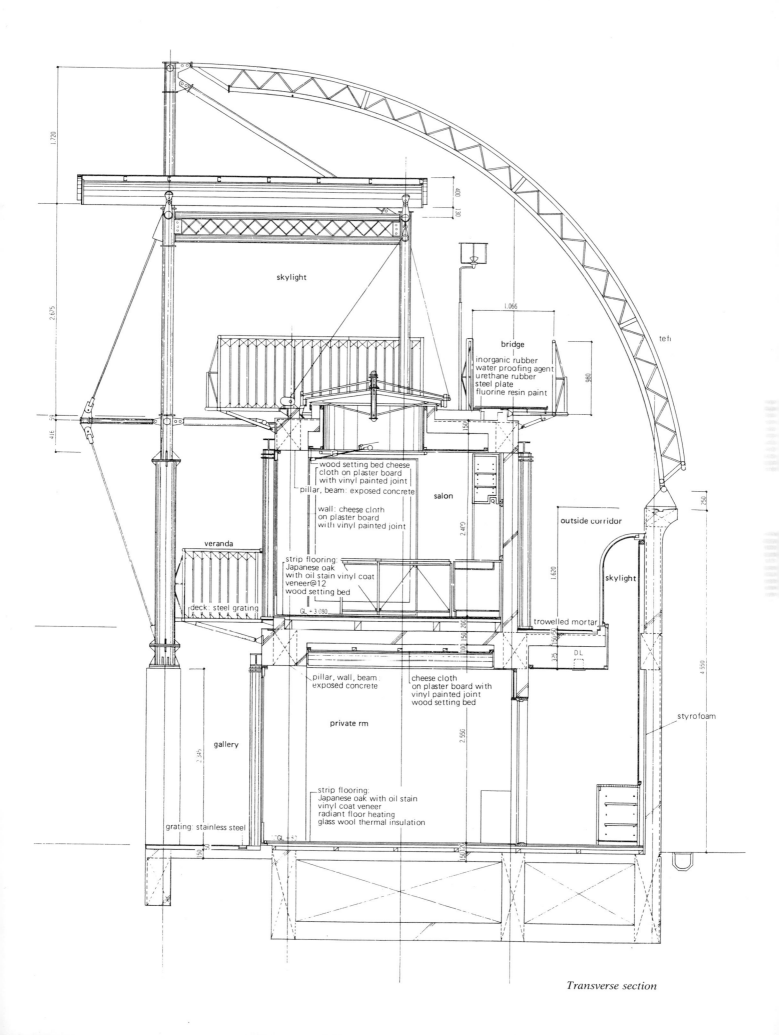

skylight

bridge
inorganic rubber
water proofing agent
urethane rubber
steel plate
fluorine resin paint

tefi

wood setting bed cheese
cloth on plaster board
with vinyl painted joint
pillar, beam: exposed concrete

wall: cheese cloth
on plaster board
with vinyl painted joint

salon

outside corridor

veranda

skylight

strip flooring:
Japanese oak
with oil stain vinyl coat
veneer@12
wood setting bed

deck: steel grating

trowelled mortar

GL + 3.080

DL

gallery

styrofoam

pillar, wall, beam:
exposed concrete

cheese cloth
on plaster board with
vinyl painted joint
wood setting bed

private rm

strip flooring:
Japanese oak with oil stain
vinyl coat veneer
radiant floor heating
glass wool thermal insulation

grating: stainless steel

GL ± 0

Transverse section

AKIRA KOMIYAMA

4th Building • Tokyo • 1986

The 4th Building is one of the latest projects realized by our studio. It is typical of the kind of multi-use building found in Tokyo: it has a restaurant in the basement, a two-tiered, ground-level retail space, two floors of office space above that, and a multi-purpose convention hall at the top. The characteristic appearance of this building derives from the combination of a cast concrete structure for the basement and ground floor and a steel structure above. Furthermore, in this architecture, structure, mask, and transparency exist side by side to create the façade. Every building has a structure

that enables it to stand up, and a face that marks it with identification. This face is normally the skin of the building and is often charged with some imagery. The imagery of the 4th Building develops from the combination of structure and face mentioned above. Despite the fashionable Tokyo location, several kinds of simple industrial materials were used on the interior. These materials, while common in one context, became quite a surprise in a fashion retail space.

Round columns lead into the building from the street side in a one-to-four incline, thus the neutrality and non-impact of per-

pendicular crosses were avoided. By opting for this diagonal line, the structure activates its surroundings and adds to it a dynamic component, much as in a Russian constructivist work. Although many architectural elements were employed and displayed, they were all articulated within an open system; and so, now each element also has connections elsewhere, outside its own system. In other words, every element is related to a larger context, thereby dissolving the singularity of architecture in the city. Therefore, this architecture is evocative of a specific urban *topos*. This type of design,

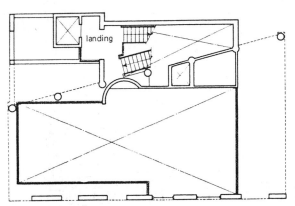

Mezzanine.

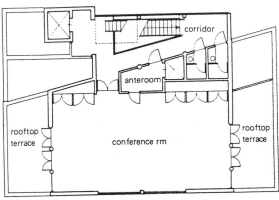

Fourth floor.

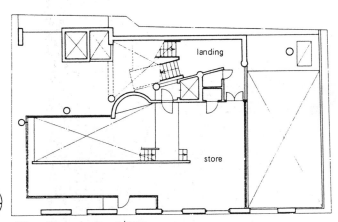

First floor; scale: 1/300.

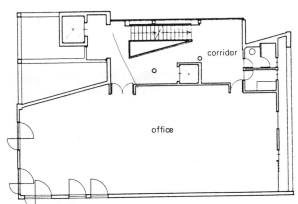

Second floor.

with no predominant form or superior order to follow and represent, could also be described as a process of de-thematization and de-architecturalization.   *A. Komiyama*

184   AKIRA KOMIYAMA

Reim Building • Tokyo • 1988

Reim is located in the midst of Shibuya in downtown Tokyo. The area is loaded with fast-food stores, bars, drug stores, and video game centers. The area is also full of neon illumination, big and small billboards, and the streets are crowded nearly 24 hours a day.

Reim could be called "a clockwork orange" rather than architecture, because what are really important to its function are the elevator and power distribution boxes. The elevator absorbs passers-by into the upper floors and dumps them back into the flow, and the power distribution boxes (located on the roof) allow all of the commerce in this building to take place.

Simple architecture would seem rather stoic in such a mass of hyperactivity. There is almost no building here, except for glazing, some steel-panel-covered structure, and emergency staircases that might interrupt the uninterrupted flow.

What I tried to do here then was neither flatten myself into the pastiche of "collage city," nor insert in it substances of a foreign sort. I tried, instead, a kind of creative tearing away from collage city. I think the will to do this has been a goal of architecture since the beginning of the modern movement. *A. Komiyama*

190   AKIRA KOMIYAMA

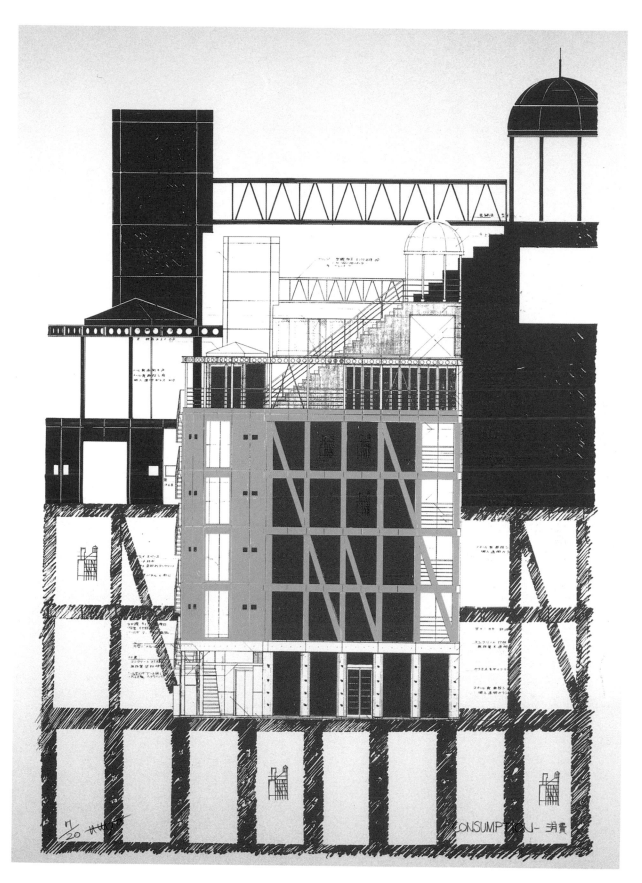

CONSUMPTION— 消費

AKIRA KOMIYAMA 191

RYOJI SUZUKI
Azabu Edge • Tokyo • 1987

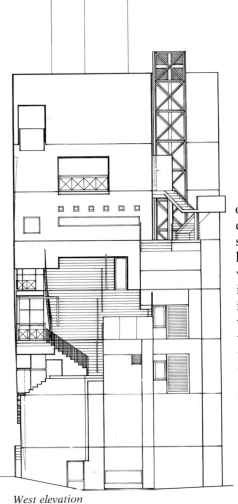

West elevation

If, as is often said to me, my architectural works have a fragmentary character, it is not because I am aiming for it; it is simply the result of the design process and thinking in which I am currently involved. At the base of such design lies a recognition of the contemporary feeling of the impossibility of anything to reach a state of completion on its own.

What really interests me is not any single value, but the kind of tensions that are produced when a plurality of values with various tendencies are able to coexist. This means an understanding of architecture not as a kind of solid entity capable of guiding disparate elements towards a synthesis, but of grasping it as a kind of center of power where various energies are free to pull in different directions. Accordingly, from the outset I would envisage the greatest possible variety and breadth in the directions that this kind of architecture might take, even though they might be mutually contradictory. This applies on the level of concepts, of structures, and even of materials. Therefore, far from wishing to intervene in order somehow to conveniently coordinate these relations of tensions, I would rather work toward mak-

ing them more vivid. This is not a process of invention, but one of discovery. In this way, I would like to continue working toward the dissolution of the framework that seeks to confine architecture to a single dogma, and at the same time I am aiming to break those closed circuits that are trying to limit me. The kind of architecture I would like to put into practice, in opposition to to-day's architecture of elaborate closed circuits, is an open one; I aim to extract the kind of power that is produced in that border-line region where fragments of radically different nature interact.

The Azabu Edge is a multi-story building that provides rental spaces for a variety of res-taurants, offices, and the like; it also includes the owner's resi-dence on the top two floors. The building is located in one of To-kyo's busiest, most fashionable districts, called Azabu, with con-gested main roads, an elevated expressway, a vehicular under-pass, and a large array of densely built, though rather nondescript structures in the immediate vi-cinity. *R. Suzuki*

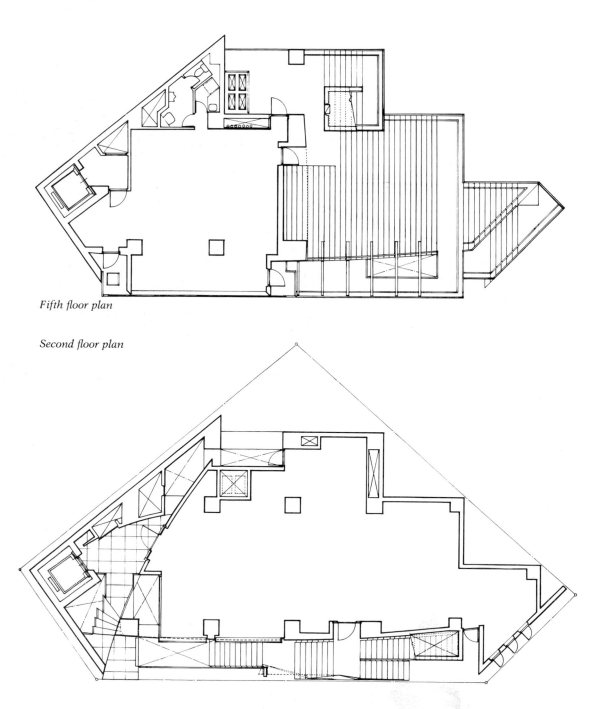

Fifth floor plan

Second floor plan

House at Honkomagome • Tokyo • 1988

There no longer exists an open world of unexpectedness or spontaneity. Ours is a world where questions and answers are paired in a one-to-one correspondence without deviating from the program, and where a complete program or closed circuit governs; this is the situation we are in at present. In principle, miracles never happen here.

If you enter the circuit with your doubts about the program turned off, the world operates very well. By repeating an extremely restricted response rule to give an answer of 0 or 1, or

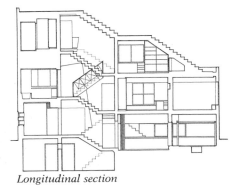

Longitudinal section

right or wrong, and by becoming inherently acquainted with this dementia reflex movement, the game proceeds at increasing speed without stagnation, and in one forward direction. By the forward movement, we mean progress of society, improvement in productivity, upgrade of performance, and growth of economy. The closed circuit that allows us to operate is driven by the accelerating force of a racing machine running at top efficiency toward the predetermined goal. By continuously fueling the engine with enthusiasm, we can gain unbe-

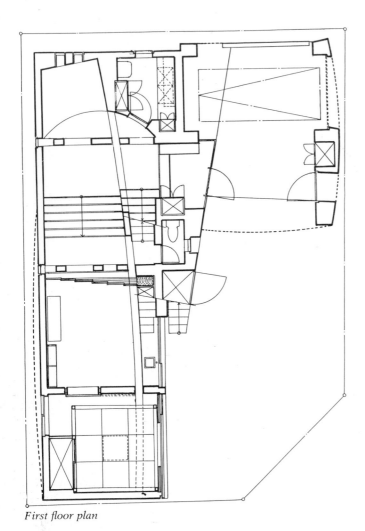

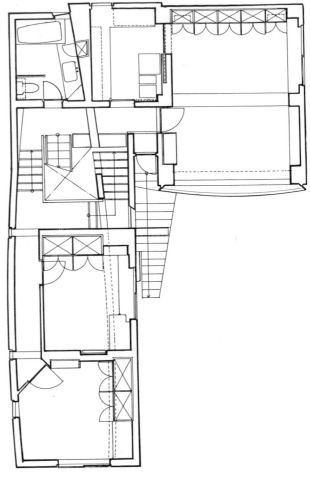

First floor plan   *Second floor plan*

lievable excitement, pleasure, and speed at the sacrifice of our field of vision; here there is no need for a pit-stop called experience.

The closed circuit, being firmly involved in architecture as well, is supported by the compromise or preestablished harmony between the primary and secondary terms, that is, between form and material, and by the one-to-one correspondence between their estimated effects and actual results. They can only function to neutralize and quell all possible dynamics within the architectural sphere. Yet, as we said, this is not only an architectural problem, but also a worldwide cultural phenomenon. Is it possible, then, to escape from the closed circuit, where even rebellion, deviation, and surprise attack are programmed in advance?

Our method, called experience in material, is an attempt to prevent this from happening; it intends to cancel the reconciliation between the primary and secondary terms. They are expected to offset each other by utilizing their opposition before they are harmonized and neutralized. It seems that an open circuit leading somewhere could be found in any interstice in the network of an apparently closed circuit. We believe that the spatial definition and experiential qualities, plus the resulting architecture of discovery represented by this house (Experience in Material No. 25) and other works of ours can achieve the opening up of deterministic, closed circuit correspondences.
R. Suzuki

SHIN TAKAMATSU

Kirin Plaza • Osaka • 1987

The mechanisms of absenting and abstracting the city, which in Shin Takamatsu's architecture operate through the incongruity of fragmentation and the anarchy of a machine vocabulary, are, in the case of the Kirin building, suspended by a strict bi-axial symmetry and uniformity of formal elements. The building, by virtue of the exactness of its form, acknowledges the city as a concrete place of architecture. However, this acknowledgement remains only a tentative proposition, insofar as it is submitted to subsequent interrogations through a manneristic manipulation of architectural form.

Here, the ambiguity of form, which bears a curious resemblance to the *andon*, a traditional Japanese floor lamp, is further reinforced by the deliberate elimination of any sense of building scale, revealing the architect's intention to de-architecturalize architecture. Consequently, the Kirin inserts itself in the urban fabric as a giant, handcrafted object creating a paradoxical situation which, in opposition to the initial proposal, questions the very reality of the city.

It would be naive to believe that such formal articulation of the building has its raison d'etre solely in Takamatsu's pursuit of

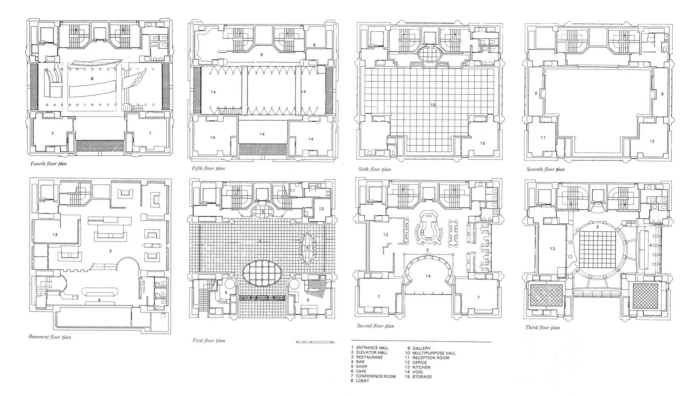

Fourth floor plan

Fifth floor plan

Sixth floor plan

Seventh floor plan

Basement floor plan

First floor plan

Second floor plan

Third floor plan

1 ENTRANCE HALL	9 GALLERY
2 ELEVATOR HALL	10 MULTIPURPOSE HALL
3 RESTAURANT	11 RECEPTION ROOM
4 BAR	12 OFFICE
5 SHOP	13 KITCHEN
6 CAFE	14 VOID
7 CONFERENCE ROOM	15 STORAGE
8 LOBBY	

freedom of beauty; clearly, it also denotes the architect's desperate attempt to save his architecture from imminent oblivion. *Andon* thus becomes the metaphor of a utilitarian object, an absolute thing in itself whose meaning, defined by its own function and utility, is self-referential and non-contextual; the Kirin represents the ultimate form of autonomous architecture devised to resist the unpredictability of its own existence within the subversive and annihilating chaos of the Japanese city. By the implied analogy of its form, the building suggests another difficult paradox: in order to be saved, architecture has to be abandoned.

Yet, on another level, Takamatsu seems to fall prey to, or accepts, the same annihilating condition imposed on him by the city he wants to resist. The mesmerizing grandeur of the Kirin's exterior stands in absurd contrast to the banality of its program. The building, owned by a major national brewery, is nothing else but an "urbanite's playhouse" that contains prosaic entertainment facilities: cocktail bar, beer pub, restaurants, exhibition gallery, and an auditorium. The articulation of the interiors indeed casts no doubt about the triviality of the world they serve. Since kitsch is no more an issue in the perverse game between urban dweller and architect, or the voyeur and the exhibitionist, the two protagonists in the urban drama of alienation, the interior spaces of the Kirin represent a stage where everybody's dreams (or nightmares) can come true.

On the other hand, the building's façade, carved with the stupefying devotion to, and enchantment with, the mysterious alchemy of its making, with its glittering blackstone surfaces, surreal in their aloofness and threatening with their unknown depths, stands in mute silence. With no real content to signify, the Kirin cannot point anywhere but towards itself—its form becomes its own content and purpose, that is, an empty sign. Takamatsu, in his determination to save architecture on a formal level, has undoubtedly refused to recognize and deal with the mechanisms which, in the context of the Japanese city, define its use and meaning. Thus, he was ultimately doomed to complete a full circle and come back to the starting point, by reinstating the same contradictory condition of architecture in which form and meaning are mutually exclusive. Can this work then serve what Roland Barthes called an "Empire of Signs? Yes, if it is understood that these signs are empty and that the ritual is without a god." In the end, Takamatsu's Kirin building becomes more credible as a monument to the absurdity of the Japanese city. *Vladimir Krstic*

ATSUSHI KITAGAWARA

Rise • Tokyo • 1986

The metropolis is, at present, generating yet another kind of gloom. It is not the gloom superimposed on the shadows of the intricately accumulated clusters of architecture, the loneliness of congested traffic, the deadly image of back streets, or office buildings in the dead of night, but the gloom of broad daylight. Accompanied by a highly refined, delightful logic, this gloom is perhaps a tedium rendered by economics, politics, authority, technology, and commodities.

For the past 100 years, the metropolis has been greatly torn between two extremes, its volition and commodities. And, tak-ing leave of space and substance, it has turned into an oscillating and accelerating tapestry without depth or thickness, and has gradually been enveloped in white gloom. In our minds, however, the metropolis is fragmentary and sublimated, though barely, into an ideal image. Reconstruction of our lost metropolis is but a futile tale, waiting to be told, for our meager imaginations can in no way stand up to the power held by metropolitan gloom. The metropolis occupies a position far greater than the one we afford it in our consciousness. And the metropolis is accelerating at a rate with which

we will never be able to compete.

More than being an architecture, Rise—a store and movie theater complex—is a fragment of the metropolis, an accumulation of the metropolis' various interiors, a reflection of the metropolis; and if the gloom of broad daylight has a king, the Rise is an evening garden enameled by his absolute, yet futile rule. *A. Kitagawara*

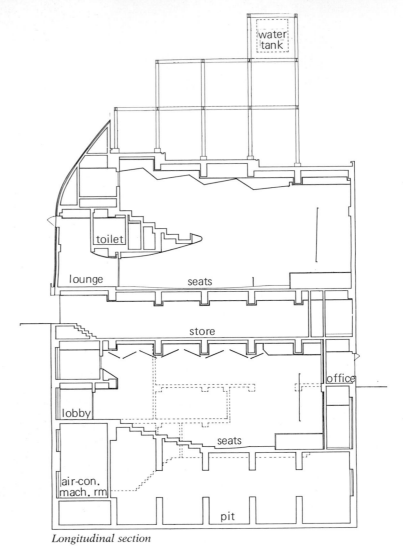

Longitudinal section

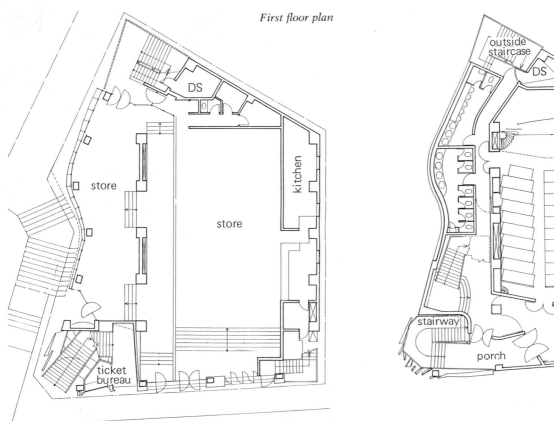

First floor plan

Second floor plan

MASAHARU TAKASAKI

Crystal Light • Tokyo • 1987

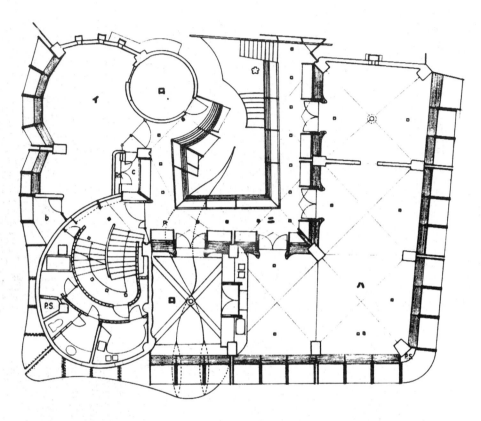

I consider architecture a social art. Architecture should be more than just what it is; a building must be more than mere shelter. Architecture must serve as a source of spirit and energy; deliberate and calculated, it focuses on nature and the human/social environment by both asking the questions and addressing the answers to the problems of the past, present, and future of human history. Architecture itself, as a great entity, along with other formative arts, should assume the responsibility of unifying the various elements of humanity and nature. If, in everyday life, architecture were to offer easy and nat-

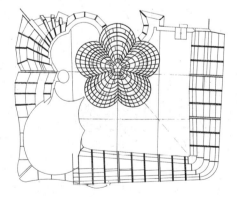

ural communication between the spiritual essence and the things of substance, it would then, in my view, fulfill its role as a social art.

Embodying architecture with such humanistic characteristics, I can now better explain this project. The exterior walls of sculptured stainless steel are my expression of environmental art. Each part is crafted with patience and energy. The north façade, however, is more humble in purpose and modest in expression, and is composed of a gentle geometry. The organic south façade takes on the task of producing a rhythmic balance and of symbolizing the concepts of life and en-

ergy. My concept is composed of two major elements: movement and repose, each to articulate the other. Movement is expressed in a parabola vertically extended into the space; the verticality expresses a statement of strength, a resolve to stand firmly on its earth base. Repose is achieved as a metaphor in horizontally flowing strata, which also function as interior storage channels. The walls of the interior court, with their highly polished surfaces of steel,

become video planes that constantly mirror the changing moods and attitudes of space, nature, and people.

The courtyard encloses the landscape just as the open ring louvers seem to "arcade" the sky. Interior spaces are glass-walled and open in all directions to receive the play of natural light and the constant dance of air and shadow. Two wooden pillars of cedar and pine stand in each entrance hall, to add points of tra-

ditional Japanese reference.

My task in this project was to provide those who will utilize this environment with a unique combination of stability and magnetism. Regardless of where they may be located within the enclosure, they will always be aware of the outside environment, feel its influences, and have as their choice the option of coexisting with nature. *M. Takasaki*

HAJIME YATSUKA

Angelo Tarlazzi • Tokyo • 1987

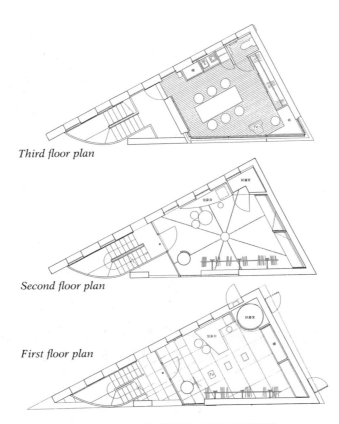

Third floor plan

Second floor plan

First floor plan

This playful building, a pilot shop for the Paris-based Italian fashion designer, Angelo Tarlazzi, is situated in the Nishi-Azabu district of Tokyo, which has recently become well-known for fashionable boutiques and restaurants. The design for the Tarlazzi shop was created through close collaboration between the interior design team, The Air, and myself.

The basic rhetorical background is composed of a black (aluminum-finished) wall with regular openings, situated at the rear of the site instead of the front. This disposition brings about the reversion of the front and back. The interplay of exte-rior and interior elements in front of the façade is the subject of this design. My intention was to make this interplay as exquisite as possible—a kind of elegant dance before a black canvas. It is as if invisible threads connect every component in the composition, setting up a subtle tension among them.

Among its components, one may find quotations from Le Corbusier's Heidi Weber Pavilion in Zurich, with some modifications. These quotations are promoted not out of snobbish historicism, but by what I once called "co-vibration with modernism." I am opposed to any kind of reaction

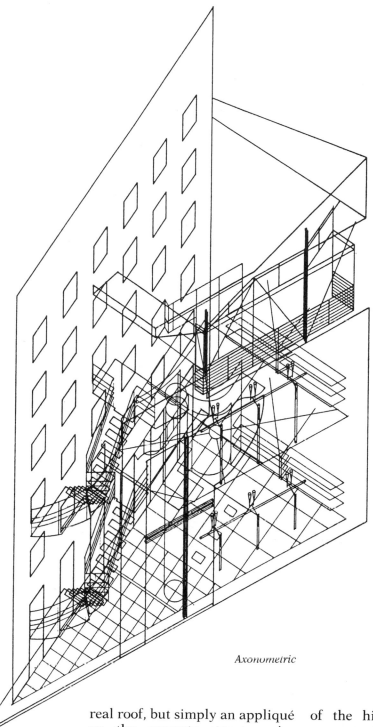

Axonometric

to modernism, such as the dull historicism and populism being advocated these days, for I believe in the possibility of developing modernist devices. I call this approach the acceleration of the modern (implying that another way is deceleration). This acceleration does not always go the same way as modernist doctrine. For instance, the quotation from Le Corbusier's work is not a real roof, but simply an appliqué on the concrete structure intended to give the impression of a light steel-frame box, like a red butterfly fluttering in front of the black background.

I am well aware that designs such as this may be somewhat annoying to those who are faithful to the monolithic unity of modernist theory. However, after investigation (perhaps I should say "archaeological investigation," as did the late Michel Foucault) of the history of the modern movement, I have become convinced that modernism never achieved real unity, and produced no more than incomplete "machines." I believe the development or the acceleration of the possibilities of modernism could never be accomplished without restructuring the old official code. Therefore "deconstruction" is inevitable here. The Tarlazzi shop is one illustration of this. *H. Yatsuka*

House in Komae · Tokyo · 1988

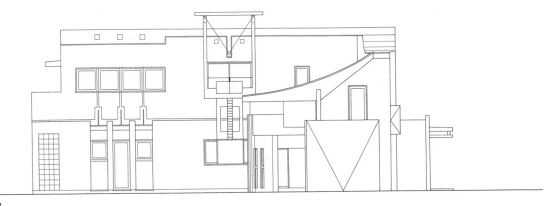

East elevation

This is an architect's private house designed with two wings that form an L-shape. The lower one, in addition to including the kitchen and dining area, features the living room with a mezzanine-level working area as the studio, all under the umbrella-shaped roof. The higher two-story wing contains the bedrooms. The former is a pavilion with a unique expression and has the same curved wall as the Maisons La Roche-Jeanneret by Le Corbusier. The latter has a more classic and stylish articulation, somewhat similar to the *fin-de-siècle* residential works of Otto Wagner and Joseph Hoffman. This paradox, namely the juxtaposition of Corbusian modernism and reinterpreted Viennese architecture from the early part of this century lends the design a diverse and dynamic impression. *H. Yatsuka*

Second floor

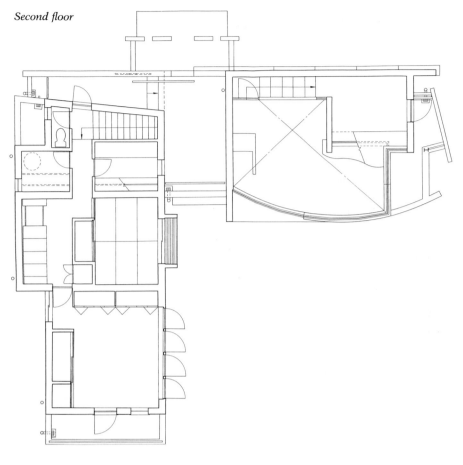

First floor

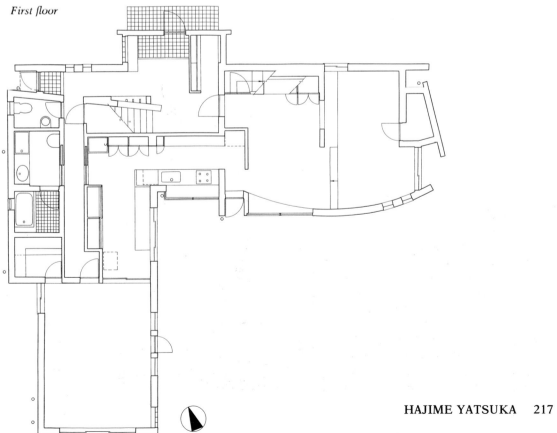

KAZUYO SEJIMA

Platform No. 1 • Katsuura • Chiba Prefecture • 1988

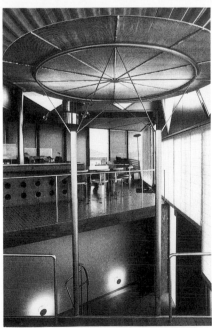

Our actions occur sequentially although they do not follow any specific sequence. Since our actions do not take place according to a prewritten scenario, nor are they directed to one destination, they are like a set of episodes in a story. Still, actions will be carried on while being separated into several different space and time segments.

Architecture can be viewed from various aspects: starting with the pragmatic, such as performance, functions, and productivity; then configuration; spatial quality; and also meaning, to name but a few. They all portray architecture as something from

which we cannot escape. Yet I would like to look at architecture in terms of its relations to *actions* that are occurring inwardly, rather than viewing it from the outside. In most cases, creating architecture means making an internal space, as a container cut out from the external space, to accommodate specific actions. In this case architecture starts out with an existing volume, which limits, if not stops, actions. I, however, consider architecture as a site or locale where a number of actions can pass by. Could architecture be a temporary phenomenon that appears in an action-maker's awareness as im-

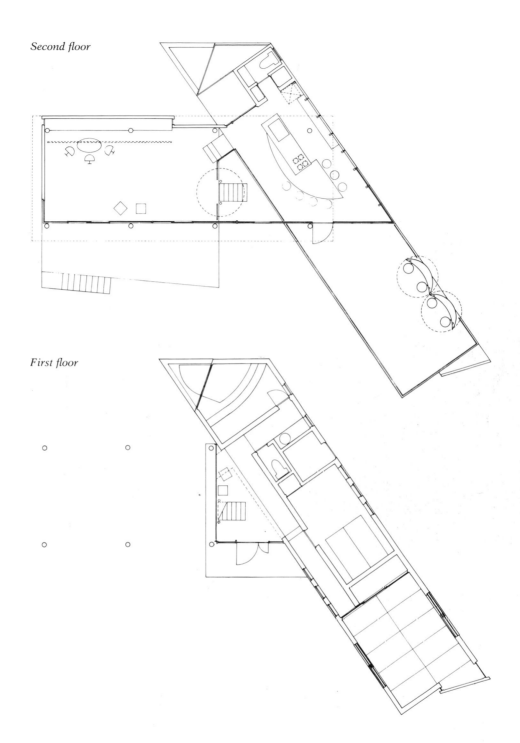

ages when actions move across the locale?

Currently, my attempt is to make architecture overlap with actions that are performed discontinuously. When such momentary actions coincide with locales, a certain volume and detectable outline are derived. An-other moment would bring a new outline. Thus a definitive, fixed image cannot precede or emerge out of the whole process. Rather, action-to-action proceeding connects separated locales, which eventually turn into a greater entity. Then, after all the actions have taken place, a locale re-sumes breathing silently; it reforms itself back into a quiet place. A locale that overlaps a number of actions of different nature must possess an innate structure in order to encompass them and to allow for their interaction. The creation of architecture in a physical sense, therefore, is a pro-

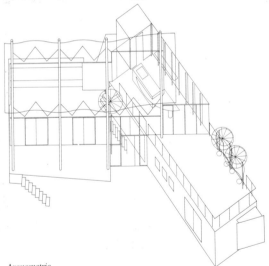

Axonometric

cess of projecting the invisible structures, which sustain those locales, into concrete construction.

Completed about a year ago, Platform No. 1 is a weekend residence with the total area of thirty-five *tsubo* (1 tsubo = 3.3 square meters). What is attempted within this house is the development of a limitlessly stretchable place and a cover that does not determine actions. For this, a series of two L-shaped frames is built with a thin, undulating roof cover that emerges like a never-ending pattern. While the wave-like roof covers the actions occurring underneath, these actions could stretch forward by crossing the frames. *K. Sejima*

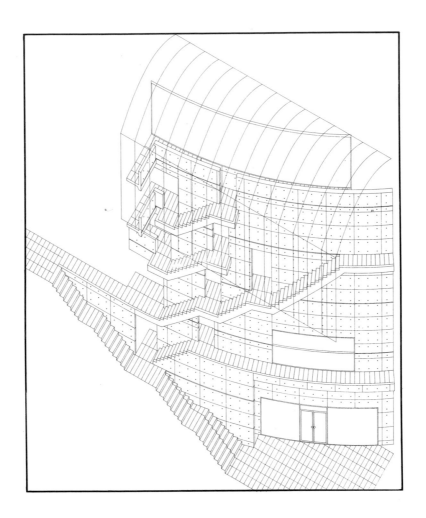

Tadao Ando, Galleria Akka, Osaka, 1988 (axonometric)